Br

Brownian movement
Bryophytes

Bu

Bubonic plague
Buckeye
Buckwheat
Bud
Buffalo
Bugs
Bulbs
Bunsen burner
Bunting
Buoy
Buoyancy
Burbank, Luther
Burnet, Sir Frank
Burns
Burro
Bursitis
Butane
Butterflies

By

Byrd, Richard E.

Ca

Cabbage
Cables
Cactus
Caddis fly
Cadmium
Caffeine
Caladium
Calamine
Calcium
Calcium carbonate
Calculator
Calendar
Calendula
Californium
Caliper
Calorie
Calorimetry
Calyx
Cambium

Camel
Camellia
Camera
Camouflage
Camphor
Canal
Canary
Cancer
Cancer (disease)
Candela
Candytuft
Canis Major
Canker sore
Canker worm
Canned heat
Canyon
Cape
Cape Canaveral
Capillary
Capricornus
Capsule
Capybara
Carat
Carbohydrates
Carbolic acid
Carbon
Carbon cycle
Carbon dioxide
Carbon life
Carbon monoxide
    tetrachloride
Carbonates
Carbonization
Carburetor
Carcinogen
Cardinal
Cardinal climber
Carnation
Carnivore
Carp
Carrier wave
Carriers
Carrot
Cartilage tissue
Cartography
Carver, George
Cashmere
Cassiopeia
Castor oil
Cat family
Catalpa
Catalyst

Cataract
Catbird
Caterpillar
Catfish
Cathode
Cathode ray
Catkin
Catnip
Cattail
Cauliflower
Caustic
Cave
Caviar
Cayenne

Ce

Cedar
Celery
Celestial navigation
Cellophane
Cells
Cellulose
Cement
Cenozoic Era
Centaurus
Centigrade
Centipede
Centrifugal forces
Centrifuge
Century plant
Cepheus
Cereal grains
Cerebellum
Cerebral palsy
Cerebrum
Cerium
Cesium
Cetacea

Ch

Chain reaction
Chalk
Chameleon
Channel
Chaparral
Charged particles
Charles' Law
Chemical change
Chemistry

Chemotherapy
Cherry
Chickadee
Chicken
Chicken pox
Chicle
Chicory
Chimpanzee
Chinchilla
Chinook Wind
Chipmunk
Chitin
Chiton
Chloride
Chlorine
Chloroform
Chlorophyll
Cholera
Cholesterol
Chordata
Chromium
Chromosomes
Chrysanthemum

Ci

Cilia
Cineraria
Cinnabar
Cinnamon
Circadian rhythm
Circulatory system
Cirrhosis
Citric acid
Citrus fruits
Civet

Cl

Clam
Clay
Cleavage
Cleft palate
Cliff
Climate
Climax community
Cloaca

YOUNG PEOPLE'S
SCIENCE ENCYCLOPEDIA

Edited by the Staff of
NATIONAL COLLEGE OF EDUCATION, Evanston, Illinois

ASSOCIATE EDITORS

HELEN J. CHALLAND, B.E., M.A., Ph.D.
  Chairman, Division of Natural Sciences
  National College of Education,
  Evanston, Illinois

DONALD A. BOYER, B.S., M.S., Ph.D.
  Science Education Consultant, Winnetka
  Public Schools, Winnetka, Illinois
  Science, National College of Education

EDITORIAL CONSULTANTS
ON THE STAFF OF NATIONAL COLLEGE OF EDUCATION

Elizabeth R. Brandt, B.A., M.Ed.
Eugene B. Cantelupe, B.A., M.F.A., Ph.D.
John H. Daugherty, B.S., M.A.
Irwin K. Feinstein, B.S., M.A., Ph.D.
Mary Gallagher, A.B., M.A., Ph.D.
Beatrice S. Garber, A.B., M.S., Ph.D.
Hal S. Galbreath, B.S. Ed., M.S.
Arthur J. Hannah, B.S., M.Ed., Ed.D.

Robert R. Kidder, A.B., M.A., Ph.D.
Jean C. Kraft, B.S., M.A., Ph.D.
Elise P. Lerman, B.A., B.F.A., M.F.A.
Mary M. Lindquist, B.A., M.A., Ph.D.
Mary-Louise Neumann, A.B., B.S.L.S.
Lavon Rasco, B.A., M.A., Ph.D.
Bruce Allen Thale, B.S.Ed., M.S.Ed.
Fred R.Wilkins, Jr., B.A., M.Ed., Ph.D.

SPECIAL SUBJECT AREA CONSULTANTS

Krafft A. Ehricke, B.A.E., H.L.D.
Benjamin M. Hair, A.B., M.D.
Charles B. Johnson, B.S., M.A., M.S.
Raymond J. Johnson, B.B.A., M.Ed.

H. Kenneth Scatliff, M.D.
Eleanor S. Segal, M.D.
Paul P. Sipiera, B.A., M.S.
Ray C. Soliday, B.A., B.S., M.A. (Deceased)

Don Dwiggins, Aviation Editor

THE STAFF

Project Director   Rudolph A. Hastedt
Project Editor   M. Frances Dyra
Senior Editor   Jim Hargrove
Editorial Assistant   Janet Zelasko

Young People's
SCIENCE
Encyclopedia

Edited by the Staff of
NATIONAL COLLEGE OF EDUCATION
Evanston, Illinois

Volume 4/Br-Cl

CHILDRENS PRESS ™

CHICAGO

Photographs

Page 2:   Skylab space station (NASA)

Page 3:   *Top to Bottom:*
          Wheatfield (U.S.D.A. Photo)
          Technician capping Abbokinase (Abbott Laboratories)
          Spider (Macmillan Science Company)
          View of Earth (NASA)
          Space Shuttle (NASA)
          Bahama coral reef (Macmillan Science Company)

Cover: Cattle (James P. Rowan)
         Oranges (Macmillan Science Co.)
         Painted lady butterfly (Jon R. Nickles:
         U.S. Fish and Wildlife Service)

Library of Congress Catalog Card Number: 67-17925

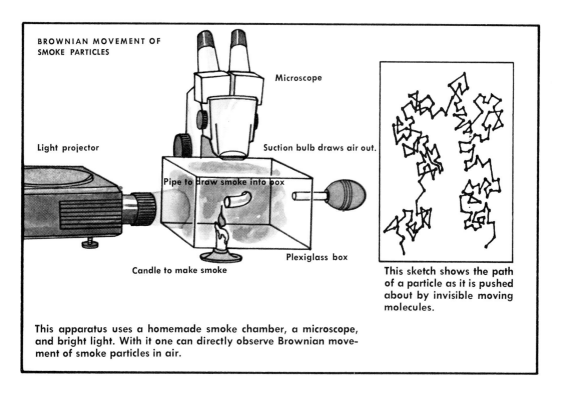

BROWNIAN MOVEMENT OF SMOKE PARTICLES

Microscope

Light projector

Suction bulb draws air out.

Pipe to draw smoke into box

Candle to make smoke

Plexiglass box

This sketch shows the path of a particle as it is pushed about by invisible moving molecules.

This apparatus uses a homemade smoke chamber, a microscope, and bright light. With it one can directly observe Brownian movement of smoke particles in air.

Brownian movement Small particles of matter (molecules) are in constant motion. This constant motion is called Brownian movement and was proven by experiment. In 1827, Robert Brown, an Englishman, put very fine powder in water. The particles moved around as though alive. Brown watched them through his microscope. He found that the movement was caused by water molecules constantly moving and hitting the powder particles. This is what happens to dust in the air when air molecules keep striking the tiny dust particles.

Brown's experiment showed that microscopic particles constantly and randomly vibrate in water or air. In 1828, Brown published his paper claiming that unknown "forces" were active in causing organic objects (bacteria and cell granules) to move. In the 1870s, after Brown's death, a new idea, the Kinetic Molecular Theory, began to gain wide scientific importance. The theory described why moving molecules collide. Only then did the deeper significance of Brownian movement come to be known. Brown's "unknown forces" were clearly explained by this new theory.

Under this theory, all matter—gas, liquid or solid—is made of invisible particles, i.e., molecules. The atoms or molecules are constantly in motion, in proportion to the temperature; and only at ABSOLUTE ZERO does all molecular motion stop.

Thus, when microscopically visible large clumps of molecules (such as dust or clusters of organic molecules) are floated in air or water, one can see the bigger particles buffeted around by the dashing water molecules, though these latter are invisible. Robert Brown's microscope and his keen eye captured this fact. Later the Kinetic Molecular Theory explained it.   D. A. B.

SEE ALSO: MOLECULAR THEORY

Brussels sprouts see Cabbage

Bryophytes (BRY-uh-fights) This is one of the 12 large plant divisions. It includes the mosses, liverworts, and horned liverworts. Most are small land plants. They have no true leaves or stems. They are held in the soil by rhizoids. They do not have conducting

Hornworts are small, lobed plants

Courtesy Society For Visual Education, Inc.
Liverworts are the simplest bryophytes

Courtesy Society For Visual Education, Inc.
Mosses are the best known bryophytes

tubes. However, some cells are similar to sieve tubes in higher plants.

Class Musci, the mosses, has about 15,000 species. At their most familiar stage, they are green and leafy. Mosses reproduce by forming multicellular *spores*. These spores develop into the leafy green gametophyte plants. Gametophytes produce both male and female cells. The fertilized egg develops into a stalk and capsule during the sporophyte generation. This stage of development is partly parasitic on the gametophyte. Mosses are found in moist places from the tropics to the polar areas.

The class Hepaticae, or liverworts, is the most primitive. There are about 8,000 species. They grow in moist shade, mainly in the tropics. Some grow as epiphytes, or non-parasitically, on trees. The plant body is a thallus. The common liverwort found in the temperate regions is called the Marchantia. The sexual organs form a head of rays on top

of a tiny stalk. The sporophyte capsule forms under the female rays.

The class Anthocerotae, or horned liverworts, includes only fifty species. The small, flat thallus is only 1 inch (2.54 centimeters) long. Horned liverworts are almost the only higher plants with pyrenoids. They are homothallic (organs of both sexes on the same plant).

In evolution Bryophytes are at a dead end. The present view is that they arose from algae but did not give rise to higher plants. It is thought that vascular plants came directly from green algae.   H.J.C.

SEE ALSO: ALTERNATIONS OF GENERATIONS

Bubonic plague (bew-BAHN-ick) Bubonic plague derives its name from the change which it causes in the human body and from the fact that it tends to strike large numbers of the population at one time. *Bubonic* means a swelling of certain glands in the body. The disease is very contagious.

The disease is spread by a flea which has been living on an infected rat. The cause of the disease is a short, rod-shaped bacterium with rounded ends called the bacillus *Yersinia (Pasteurella)*. When a person is infected, painful swelling of the glands in the groin, armpits, and neck develops. These swellings vary from the size of a walnut to a goose egg. They can swell until they burst and become open sores (the "buboes" from which the plague gets its name). Black-and-blue spots sometimes found on the body gave rise to the term BLACK DEATH. Actually, these spots are hemorrhages resulting from the plague's deadly toxin that affects the blood's ability to clot.

Bubonic plague victims develop a high temperature after one or two days. People who develop PNEUMONIA (Pneumonic plague) are almost sure to die, and the overall death rate is high in an epidemic. Plague is a problem wherever there are rats, and to prevent it the rats must be destroyed.

The early use of ANTIBIOTICS has cut down the death rate from this disease. For those who travel in countries where the disease is present, a vaccine made from cultures of the germ has been developed.   E.S.S./H.K.S.

SEE ALSO: BLACK DEATH

Buckeye tree

Buckeye The leaf of this tree is made of five to seven leaflets. Large buds grow on the ends of the branches. The many small flowers are on an upright stalk.

The leaves are palmately compound but pinnately veined. Flowers form a compound inflorescence. Each bloom lacks symmetry. The fruit is a capsule which splits down three seams. It encloses one or three seeds.

The Ohio buckeye, 40 feet (12.19 meters) high, has yellow flowers and thorns on the fruit. The sweet buckeye, 90 feet (27.43 meters) high, has a smooth fruit. The red buckeye is a small tree with red blossoms. They belong to the Sapindaceae family, also called Soapberry.   H.J.C.

Buckwheat Buckwheat is a green leafy plant. Its three-sided seeds are ground to make flour. It is not related to wheat or to other grains which belong to the grass family.

Buckwheat has a smooth, branching stem that grows from 2 to 4 feet (.61 to 1.22 meters) high. The flowers are white to pink in color and the seed has a dry papery fruit wall. The white endosperm of the seed contains more starch than other grains.

Buckwheat grows in a temperate climate which has cool, moist summers. It grows well even in poor sandy soil. A special honey is often extracted from the flower. The plant is also a source of *rutin,* used in treating circulatory disorders.   H. J. C.

Buckwheat

Leaf buds will form new stems and branches

Bud Buds are growths on stems and contain tiny leaves or flowers. They are protected by scales. They may be active (growing) or dormant (resting before growth). Buds can best be observed by collecting twigs of trees or shrubs. By placing these in water in a warm place during the early spring, their regular spring growth can be watched.

A lengthwise cut through a winter bud will show the growing tip of the stem, the young leaves and the hard outer scales. These scales may be coated with RESIN or with short, dense hairs. They serve to protect the inner parts from drought.

The *terminal bud* at the tip of the stem is responsible for elongation of the stem. A hormone is produced by this bud which suppresses the growth of the lateral buds down on the stem. This suppression of growth is most striking in firs and spruces which show a strong central stem.

Buds may be located alternately on the stem, or they may be opposite each other. In either case their position on the stem marks the *node*. The space between adjacent buds is the *internode*.

Buds develop in the *leaf axils* (angles where the stem of a leaf joins a branch). Even after the leaf has fallen, a scar remains just below the bud.

As buds become active in the spring, the stem between the young leaves elongates considerably. However, the stem between the bud scales grows very little. For this reason, the fallen scales leave a distinct ring around the twig which marks the beginning of each year's growth. The age of a young twig may be determined by counting the number of rings.

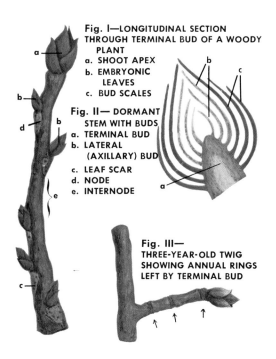

Fig. I—LONGITUDINAL SECTION
THROUGH TERMINAL BUD OF A WOODY
PLANT
a. SHOOT APEX
b. EMBRYONIC
LEAVES
c. BUD SCALES

Fig. II— DORMANT
STEM WITH BUDS
a. TERMINAL BUD
b. LATERAL
(AXILLARY) BUD
c. LEAF SCAR
d. NODE
e. INTERNODE

Fig. III—
THREE-YEAR-OLD TWIG
SHOWING ANNUAL RINGS
LEFT BY TERMINAL BUD

Buds vary greatly in appearance from the eyes of the POTATO tuber, which are really *lateral* buds, to the familiar CABBAGE head, which is a *terminal* bud.

In addition to producing stems, leaves, and flowers, buds develop growth substances which affect the whole plant.   M. D. F.

SEE ALSO: BOTANY, BULBS, PLANT

Budding see Reproduction, asexual

Buffalo Buffalo are actually bison. True buffalo are Old World animals, lacking the shoulder hump present in the bison. Bison occur in both North America and Europe. They are a kind of wild ox.

At one time, bison herds numbered in the thousands. Today both the European and American bison are scarce. They are found either in zoos or on protected ranges.

The bison's coat is woolly and dark brown. Hair on the head is long, and the animal has a beard. Its tail is short-haired with a tassel at the tip.

The bison is a very large animal with a massive head. On the head are the hollow horns characteristic of all members of the cattle family. The horns, present in both sexes, are formed around a core of bone and are never shed. Horns, round and curved, grow longer each year. The shoulder hump is formed by the long dorsal spines on the vertebrae.

On each foot, bison have two main hooves and two extra hooves. Like all cud chewers, the stomach has several compartments.

Bison calves are born in the spring or early summer. The gestation period is nine months. Normally only one yellowish calf is born each year. The females have four mammary glands for feeding the calf. The calf develops its hump in about two weeks. Young females do not breed until they are about three years old.

Bison are grazing animals that eat prairie grasses. They frequently destroy young trees by using them as scratching posts. Bison enjoy dust bathing, accomplished by rolling in the dust on the prairies. This behavior gives them relief from insect bites and prickly seeds. When bison shed, parts of their hindquarters become bare.

Many years ago, bison lived in large herds, moving south across America as they grazed. They wintered in the warm south. As the settlers moved west, they killed off the herds, and almost caused their extinction.   J. C. K.

SEE ALSO: ARTIODACTYLA

Water buffalo of Indo-China
Chicago Natural History Museum

American bison
Chicago Natural History Museum

Bugs All insects are not bugs, but all bugs are insects. There are over twenty groups of insects, and the true bugs make up only one of these groups. Bugs' wings are thick at the base near the body but thin and delicate at the ends. There may be a diamond-shaped pattern on the thorax. These are the easiest things to look for in telling bugs from all the other insects.

Bugs vary in size, but they all have sucking mouth parts with sharp beaks. They have a pair of compound eyes and often two simple eyes. They develop gradually from egg to nymph to adult. This is called *incomplete* METAMORPHOSIS. Bugs live on land, in the water, or on plants. Some bugs even live on other animals. They can make sounds by rubbing their legs and wings against other parts of their bodies.

The *aquatic bugs* live in ponds and streams, while a few are marine. They are *predaceous,* which means they attack other insects, snails, and small fish. The *water striders* take advantage of the SURFACE TENSION of the water to keep them afloat. They travel at a remarkable pace. The *back-swimmers* do just that—swim on their back, but they can also fly. Their backs resemble the bottom of a boat, and their third pair of legs serves as paddles. The *water boatmen* swim about in a crazy fashion. They eat algae and diatoms. In turn, the Mexican Indians eat them. The *giant waterbugs* are so large that they will readily attack frogs, salamanders, and fish four times larger than themselves. Their bites may cause rather painful swelling. They are called *electric-light bugs* since they are attracted to light. They hibernate in the adult stage.

The *stinkbugs* have two glands on the thorax which give off an unpleasant odor. However, birds are not bothered by this and do not hesitate to consume stink bugs in great quantities. These bugs are green or brown. They suck plant juices and are destructive to garden crops. The *harlequin* (meaning "clown") is a gaily colored bug

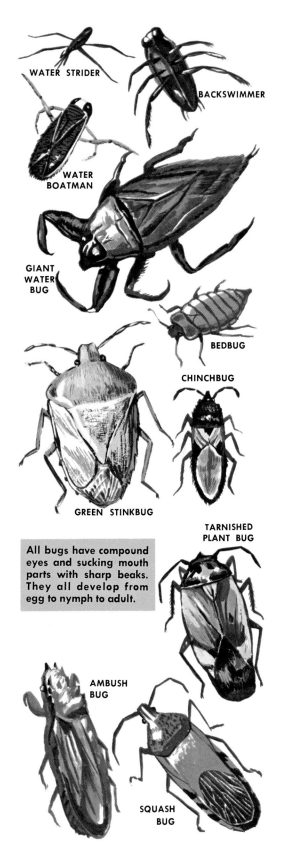

WATER STRIDER

BACKSWIMMER

WATER BOATMAN

GIANT WATER BUG

BEDBUG

CHINCHBUG

GREEN STINKBUG

TARNISHED PLANT BUG

All bugs have compound eyes and sucking mouth parts with sharp beaks. They all develop from egg to nymph to adult.

AMBUSH BUG

SQUASH BUG

that is a pest because it destroys garden plants such as radishes, turnips, and cabbage.

Bedbugs feed on birds and mammals. They are nocturnal, sneaking out of crevices and attacking their prey at night. The eggs of these bugs take two months to develop into adults. Since a pair of bedbugs may have three or four generations a year, they continue to be pests.

Chinch bugs came to America from the tropics. Since their natural enemies were left behind, they have become pests. In grain fields they destroy millions of dollars worth of grain annually. Nymphs are red, and adults gray and brown. The female lays 500 eggs two or three times a year.

Squash bugs have a strong odor. They feed on melons, gourds, and pumpkins. *Ambush bugs* are known for their bizarre forms and feeding habits. They jump from their hiding places and grab their victims with mouthparts that tear and suck.

Lace bugs have a delicate front pair of wings that look like fine lace. They have black bodies, a white underside, pale yellow legs, and antennae. These insects attack sycamore trees causing the leaves to drop.

Assassin bugs suck the blood of other insects. They can also give people a painful bite. They are sometimes referred to as "kissing bugs." Their dark brown bodies vary in shape and size.

Red bugs are real pests on cotton plants. They have a drab to bright red body with large eyes.

Cone-nosed bugs are dangerous. They carry a one-celled animal that causes the Chagas disease, common in Central and South America.

There are 55,000 species of true bugs. Not everything that crawls is a "bug." The ladybug, June bug, and lightning bug, for example, are BEETLES and not true bugs.

H.J.C.

SEE ALSO: APHIDS, INSECTA

Waterbug   Macmillan Science Co.

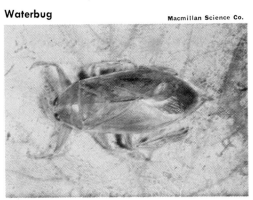

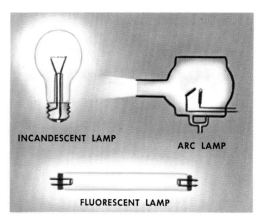

INCANDESCENT LAMP   ARC LAMP

FLUORESCENT LAMP

Bulb, electric An electric light bulb is a lamp which produces visible and invisible light by means of an electric current passing through its circuit. Electric lights may be classified as one of three types: 1) arc lamp, 2) incandescent lamp, and 3) vapor lamp.

ARC LAMP

Two carbon ELECTRODES with a small space or gap between them form the light-producing portion of the electrical circuit. When a current flows, an electric arc flashes in the gap and produces a brilliant white light. The arc lamp was rapidly replaced with the incandescent lamp as the latter became more dependable.

INCANDESCENT LAMP

This lamp is commonly called "the electric light bulb." It consists of three main parts: (a) the glass bulb or envelope, (b) the filament, and (c) the base. The bulb contains the metal filament (a fine wire) in a VACUUM or inert gas. The base seals the bulb and provides a means of passing the electric current through the filament. As the current flows, the filament becomes heated and produces light. The vacuum or inert gas enables the filament to glow more intensely than it would in ordinary air. Although the incandescent lamp which used a platinum wire and glass tube was invented in the early 19th century, it was not until 1879 that THOMAS EDISON produced the first practical lamp. His lamp consisted of a carbonized cotton thread for a filament which was operated in a high vacuum. In 1880, Joseph Wilson Swan developed the hermetically-sealed (air-tight) enclosure which is now used.

✳ THINGS TO DO

TURNING ELECTRICAL ENERGY INTO LIGHT ENERGY

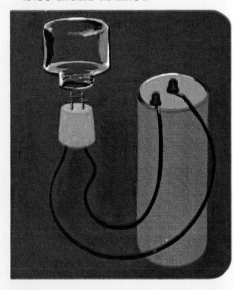

1 Push two exposed ends of bell wire through a cork. Wrap fine wire around the end of one wire, then across and around the second wire. This will be the filament in a home-made light bulb.

2 Insert the cork into the mouth of an ink bottle. Connect the other ends of the wire to a series of dry cells.

3 When the circuit is complete the filament will glow. Eventually the filament burns up since there is oxygen in the bottle. The oxygen has been removed in commercial bulbs.

Filament materials constantly were improved as they were changed from carbonized cotton and paper to bamboo to cellulose to metallized carbon. In 1907, the first TUNGSTEN filament lamp was marketed. Because tungsten was so fragile, a method of making it ductile had to be developed. Inert gases retard filament oxidation and, therefore, replaced the vacuum. By coiling the filament, the light efficiency was improved even more.

VAPOR LAMP

The commonest type of vapor lamp is a long gas-filled tube coated inside with a whitish chemical called a *phosphor*. At each end are wire contacts with inwardly-project-

ing, short tungsten wires. As the tube is turned on, an initial high voltage from a *starter* coil sends current between the end wire electrodes. In so doing, it makes the gas and the phosphor lining glow—become *fluorescent*—hence the name for these tubes. After starting, the regular 120 volts are enough to keep the tube lit. These lamps give more light and less heat than other types. Special phosphors are used to give a variety of desired effects, as "warm" or "cool" whites. One new kind gives light for indoor sprouting of seeds; another is suited to maturing of plants with little or no sunlight. Such lamps offer a new boon to greenhouse experimenters and to window-garden hobbyists.

Mercury and sodium lamps are two types of high-intensity vapor lamps which operate very efficiently, with approximately 55 lumens per watt. A third electrode is used in the mercury lamp to start the current flow. The globe contains argon gas and a small amount of mercury.

The sodium lamp is built like a vacuum bottle since it has a double-walled envelope. Two sets of electrodes are used to conduct current through the metallic sodium and neon gas contents. The sodium vapor lamp produces a yellow light making it more desirable for outdoor than indoor use.   E. I. D.

SEE ALSO: ARC, LIGHT

Edison's original bulb had sewing thread as the filament. It burned for about forty hours

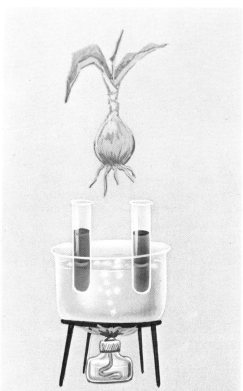

The presence of sugar and starch in a bulb can be easily tested. One-fourth teaspoon juice from a bulb is placed in a test tube containing one tablespoon of Benedict's solution. After being heated in a water bath, the liquid will turn orange if sugar is present. For the starch test, a portion of a bulb is crushed into a tablespoon of water. A few drops of iodine will turn the liquid purple if starch is present

Bulbs These are one of the four kinds of UNDERGROUND STEMS. The flat, disklike stem has fibrous roots. The leaves of the plant store the food. They contain sugar rather than starch.

Bulbs may be biennials or perennials. The fleshy leaves under the ground are white. As they grow above the surface, CHLOROPHYLL is produced. Vegetative parts above the soil die each year.

The onion is a biennial whose strong odor is derived from a sulfur compound. Garlic bulbs are made of several bulbils or "cloves." Perennial bulbs include tulip, snowdrop, and narcissus. H. J. C.

SEE ALSO: PHOTOSYNTHESIS, STEM

Bullet see Projectiles, Weapons

Bullhead see Catfish

Bunsen burner The Bunsen burner is a gas burner that gives a very hot flame. The burner consists of a metal tube on a base connected to a gas supply. Holes near the bottom permit air to mix with gas. Gas stoves work the same way.

A burner flame has three parts. The center is a gas and air mixture. In the next section the gases are partially oxidized to form carbon monoxide and carbon. In the blue or outside layer, the carbon monoxide and carbon are converted to CARBON DIOXIDE. When air is limited, the flame is yellow, due to hot carbon particles. A.J.H./J.H.D.

Bunsen, Robert Wilhelm (1811-1899) Bunsen was a German chemist who, with G. Kirchhoff, invented the SPECTROSCOPE. Bunsen used the spectroscope to study the lights of different flames.

With the spectroscope Bunsen studied the chemicals of the earth and sun. While working with some mineral water, he found some spectral lines never seen before. Concentration of 360,000,000 grams of the water yielded 17 grams of the chlorides of two new elements, rubium and cesium.

Bunting (BUN-ting) Buntings belong to a family of seed-eating birds with thick, cone-shaped bills. This family of about 700 species includes the FINCHES, CARDINALS, and GROSBEAKS. The *Indigo* bunting is completely blue. The *Lazuli* is blue with white and chestnut markings. *Painted* and *varied* buntings have mixtures of brilliant colors. All of them are found in western North America.

Painted bunting

Lighted buoy

Buoy A buoy is an anchored, floating object which marks channels or danger spots in a body of water. It may contain bells or lights as additional warning signals.

SEE: BUOYANCY

Buoyancy Buoyancy is that force which allows objects to float in liquids and in the air. When a swimmer floats on his back in the water he is using the law of buoyancy. When a BALLOON floats in the air for a period of time this is also buoyancy.

An object submerged in a liquid, such as water, weighs less than it does in air. Water applies force to the object on all sides. The bottom of the object, being deeper in the water, has a greater force on it. This difference in force is the buoyant or upward force. If the upward force is less than the weight of the object, the object sinks. If the buoyant force is greater than its weight, the object floats.

The force produced by an object is its weight. When the object is placed in water it displaces an equal volume of water. The force of the water displaced is its weight. *Archimedes' principle* expresses this as "the buoyant force of a body in a fluid is equal to the weight of the fluid displaced by the body."

Buoyancy explains why a boat can stay afloat on the water without sinking. It also explains why a SUBMARINE must carefully take on extra water in its tanks in order to submerge below the surface of the water. In order to float, the floating object must have a lower average DENSITY than the liquid which is holding it afloat. Since density means the mass of a material in a certain volume, one can easily understand how a cupful of iron would sink, while a cupful of cork would float in water. The iron is very much heavier per cupful than water, while the cork is lighter per cupful

✳ THINGS TO DO

TESTING THE BUOYANCY OF A GAS

1 Fasten a small cardboard carton to each end of a stick with a piece of string. Hold the stick in the center by a third string. Pour any soda-water beverage into a deep pan or pail.
2 Hold one carton in the pan but do not let it touch the liquid. The carton will rise.
3 The carton containing air displaces a certain amount of carbon dioxide gas. Therefore, the carton is buoyed up by a force equal to the weight of the gas it has displaced.

than water. A stone will sink in water, but is buoyed up by a force equal to the weight of the water displaced. The weight of the stone is greater than the buoyancy force upward, so it sinks.

Buoyancy applies to lighter-than-air craft such as balloons and blimps and other AIRSHIPS. These floating objects are filled with gases such as helium which have a very low density and therefore give the balloons an overall lower density than the air surrounding it.   M. S.

SEE ALSO: ARCHIMEDES

Luther Burbank

Burbank, Luther (1849-1926) Burbank was a plant breeder who learned how to develop varieties of plants and improve old ones. He was one of the first Americans to do this.

When Luther was a boy in Lancaster, Massachusetts, Darwin's theory of EVOLUTION was still very controversial in this country. Burbank seized upon it eagerly. He wanted to speed up the process of evolution in plants. Natural selection depends upon wind and insects to carry the pollen from one plant to another. He selected the best plants and took pollen from one flower to place upon another. By using only the strongest plants, or the ones that had other desirable qualities, such as sweet fruit or large blooms, he would get superior plants from their seeds. By saving only the best of the seedlings and throwing away the others, he kept on improving the strain.

He also fertilized one plant with pollen from another of a different but related species. By crossing the apricot with the Japanese plum, he produced the *plumcot*. The *Shasta daisy* was the result of crossings between the American wild daisy, the English daisy and the Japanese daisy. M.R.B.

SEE ALSO: HORTICULTURE, HYBRIDIZATION

Burnet, Sir Frank MacFarlane

(1899-1985) The 1960 NOBEL PRIZE in physiology or medicine was awarded to Burnet and Medawar. Their work in immunology led to the concept of *tolerance.*

Both tolerance and immunity involve antigen-antibody reactions of cells. These reactions are very important in the treatment of disease. The success of tissue and organ transplants depends on tolerance and immunity. The mechanisms of tolerance are not yet clearly understood. A.J.H.

SEE ALSO: ANTIBODY

Burns A burn is an injury usually caused by heat or fire. *First-degree* burns make the outermost layer of skin red and sore. Blisters form on the skin in *second-degree burns.* A *third-degree* burn destroys deeper tissue. Many major burn injuries are combinations of all three types. Electricity and strong chemical ACIDS AND BASES can also cause burns.

A person on fire should immediately drop to the ground and start rolling. A rug or blanket will also help smother the flames. Burns lessen or destroy the skin's ability to resist INFECTION. Care must be taken to avoid infections in all types of burn wounds. Minor burns should be flooded with clean, cold water until the pain is reduced. The burned area should be washed gently with soap and water and covered with a sterile gauze. Until it heals, the burn should be kept clean.

Victims of all but very minor burns should get immediate medical help. A doctor should be called if the burn is deep or large, if there is charring or swelling or blistering of the skin, if the victim develops a FEVER, if pus drains around the burn or a bad odor develops, or if the victim has not had a TETANUS shot in the last five to ten years.

Burns caused by strong chemicals should also be flooded with cold, clean water. A doctor should be called immediately. If possible, the doctor should be told the name of the chemical involved. Acid burns are often treated by washing the wound with bicarbonate of soda (baking soda) mixed in water. Alkali (base) burns can be treated with a dilute mixture of water and vinegar.

Too much exposure to the sun can also cause dangerous and painful burns. Frequent sunburns and deep tans can eventually lead to skin CANCER. V.V.N./J.H.

SEE ALSO: FIRST AID; RADIATION, PROTECTION; RAY, ULTRAVIOLET; SUNBURN

Burro A burro is a small, strong, sure-footed DONKEY. It can carry heavy loads for its size.

Spaniards brought these stubborn little donkeys to Mexico and America during the Spanish colonial days. The word "burro" is the Spanish word for donkey. They became so valuable to the Mexican Indians as pack

Burro

animals that many were kept as pets. Burros are still used in parts of Mexico to carry pottery, firewood, and heavy loads. D.J.A.

Bursitis Bursitis is a painful inflammation of a fluid-filled membrane sac (bursa) which usually forms in areas of the body where bones and tendons rub.

Bursitis can be *acute,* secondary to overuse, injury, or infection. Treatments include ANTIBIOTICS, rest of the affected area, or anti-inflammatory pills, such as aspirin. Bursitis can also be *chronic,* because of calcium deposits in the bursa. Mild exercises and aspirin help relieve chronic bursitis. In some cases CORTISONE is given or an operation is performed to relieve severe pain. E.S.S.

Bushmaster see Snakes

Butane (BU-tane). Butane is a colorless, odorless gas, used as fuel. It is found in NATURAL GAS. Butane is in the METHANE family of gases.

Butane is an organic compound. The chemical formula for butane is C_4H_{10}. There are two ways to arrange butane atoms. The first arrangement has all the carbon atoms in a single chain. This is called normal or n-butane. The second way has three carbons bonded together to form a branched chain. These two forms of butane are called *isomers.*

Butane under pressure is converted to a liquid. In its liquid state it is easily transported and stored. When the pressure is removed it returns to a gas and can be used as a fuel. A.J.H.

Buttercup There are about twelve hundred different kinds of buttercups. Some grow wild. Many others are found blooming in flower gardens.

They grow best in cooler parts of the North Temperate Zone.

Wild buttercups have glossy yellow flowers. The leaves have deep notches. They have a poisonous, acid juice.

Garden flowers belonging to the buttercup family may have symmetrically shaped flowers as do the PEONY, anemone, and love-in-a-mist. Others, such as columbine, monkshood and larkspur, bear flowers which are irregular or one-sided in shape. I. H. S.
SEE ALSO: WILD FLOWERS

Bulb buttercup

Butterflies Some of the most beautiful animals in the world are butterflies. They have long slender bodies and two pairs of wings. There are several ways the insect hunter can tell a butterfly from a MOTH. The feelers (antennae) of the butterfly are thin with knobs on the ends. The moths' antennae are feathery. The butterfly flies in the daytime and, when resting, will fold its wings up like a sail of a boat. The moth usually flies at night and, when resting, spreads its wings like those of an airplane.

Butterflies go through a complete change from egg to adult. The female lays eggs on plants which will be the food for the young larvae. The LARVA is called a CATERPILLAR. It does not form a cocoon; instead the resting stage is a *chrysalis.* The insect is a chrysalis through winter, then it becomes an adult. Most butterflies produce one brood a year.

WHAT BUTTERFLY WILL IT BE?

The orange sulphur feeds on clover

The black swallowtail is identified by the double row of yellow spots

1. Collect caterpillars or the chrysalises of several species of butterflies. Note the leaves of the plants where they are found. This is their food.
2. Place them in a container and leave it outside through the winter months. If they are brought inside in the fall the adult butterfly will emerge around December when no food is available.
3. In the early spring transfer the chrysalis to an insect cage. Supply them with fresh leaves (each species prefers certain plants).
4. Set them free when the study and observation of their life cycle has been completed.

The cosmopolite has scaly wings

The *swallowtail* butterflies are among the largest—the giant swallowtail has a wing spread from 4 to 6 inches (10.16 to 15.24 centimeters). They have "tails" projecting from the end of the wings. The larvae give off a musky odor which protects them from being eaten. The caterpillars enjoy the plant leaves like carrots and parsnips. Some will feast in citrus orchards. After nine days in a chrysalis, the adults appear, usually in beautiful black and yellow attire.

The *monarch,* or milkweed, butterfly is one of the most common and interesting butterflies in North America. The adult lays pale green eggs on the leaves of milkweed. The caterpillar has distinctive black and yellow stripes. It sheds its skin four times as it grows and molts. It is one of the few insects that migrates regularly. Monarchs leave their northern summer homes in large groups and will fly hundreds of miles to a southern habitat. They return one by one in the spring. It is not certain whether the ones returning north in the spring are the old adults or new young ones.

There are over 10,000 species in the U.S.A. and Canada, classified into many groups. The *fritillaries* comprise one of the largest groups. The caterpillars are spiny in appearance and feed at night on violets and goldenrod. The adults are distinguished by their much shortened front legs.

The group called *buckeyes* are so named because of the prominent eyespots on their wings. They have brown chrysalises, and the adults inhabit the open fields. On a beautiful summer day it is fun to try to identify these beautiful insects: the red admiral, the painted lady or thistle butterfly, the cabbage and alfalfa butterflies, the coppers, the blues, and the hairstreak varieties.   H. J. C.

SEE ALSO: INSECTA, METAMORPHOSIS

All photos Courtesy Society For Visual Education, Inc.

The cabbage butterflies are common in the U.S.

Western swallowtail has a slim smooth body

The aphrodite fritillary, like all fritillaries, is a brush-footed butterfly

Pearl crescent   Meadow fritillary

Monarch butterflies migrate like birds

Admiral Richard E. Byrd

Byrd, Richard Evelyn

Byrd, Richard Evelyn (1888–1957) Byrd was an American explorer, aviator, and naval officer. He was the first person to fly over both the North and South poles, and he did much to develop important devices and methods of navigation.

Born in Winchester, Virginia, on October 25, 1888, Richard E. Byrd attended the Virginia Military Academy and the University of Virginia. He then studied at the U.S. Naval Academy, graduating in 1912. Following graduation, he served four years in the navy and then entered aviation service.

In 1925 Byrd went on the first of his many expeditions. He served as flight commander with the MacMillan expedition to Greenland. For the first time planes were used in arctic exploration. The following year, on May 9, Byrd and Floyd Bennett flew to the North Pole and returned in fifteen and one-half hours. One year later, in July of 1927, Byrd, with another pilot and two navigators, attempted to fly across the Atlantic Ocean, but they were forced down at sea and rescued after a terrifying experience.

In 1928 Byrd organized a scientific expedition to ANTARCTICA. Accompanying him were thirty-two scientists, specialists in the fields of aerology, geography, geology, meteorology, physics, radio engineering, and topography. These specialists took with them the most elaborate equipment ever used in exploration. For Byrd's enormous contribution to science, the U.S. Congress bestowed on him the rank of rear admiral.

Between 1933 and 1935 Byrd continued a scientific survey of the Antarctic continent. In 1939 he returned to explore 900 miles of coastline around Marie Byrd Land.

To acquaint others with his polar adventures, Byrd wrote *Alone, Skyward, Little America,* and *Discovery.*   D. H. J.

Cabbage Cabbage is a leafy plant which is eaten as a vegetable. It is made into a salad when shredded raw, or may be boiled, or pickled for sauerkraut. Cabbage heads look like huge buds growing on top of short stalks. The heads may be round, oblong, flat, or cone-shaped.

Cabbage seeds may be sown in flat boxes during February or March and kept in a cool room. The seedlings should be kept moist and transplanted as they grow larger. After the danger of frost is past, the cabbage plants can be set outside in the garden. Cabbage should be raised in well-drained soil, properly enriched with plant food. It takes about one hundred days for cabbage to mature. Late varieties of cabbage should be set out in the garden about August first.

Other varieties of cabbage are red cabbage, CAULIFLOWER, Brussels sprouts, broccoli, and kale. M.R.L.

Cables A cable is a ropelike object usually made from strands of wire or, more recently, glass fibers. Cables can be divided into two groups: mechanical cables and transmission cables.

Mechanical cables are strong. They are usually made of strands of wire. They support BRIDGES, lift and lower elevators, and tow heavy loads. Transmission cables generally carry electricity or electrical signals. Fiber-optic cables carry signals made by light.

Mechanical cables are used to exert FORCE on stationary or moving objects. Mechanical cables are usually made from a number of smaller wires twisted together. Larger cables have groups of wires twisted around a core, which may be made of wires or fibers typically found in rope.

There are many different types of transmission cables. Electric power lines carry ELECTRICITY on overhead cables or in cables buried underground. Because it is an excellent electrical CONDUCTOR, COPPER or a copper ALLOY is often used in power lines. Some overhead lines in the U.S. carry powerful electric currents, up to 765,000 volts. In recent years, evidence has been found suggesting a health risk due to RADIATION from very high-power lines.

TELEPHONE lines are cables that transmit signals over sometimes vast distances. The signals can be used to transmit voices or the data used by computers. Some telephone lines, including all older ones, use electricity to transmit signals. These cables are usually made of many small copper wires. Recently, some telephone companies have begun using cables made of hair-thin strands of glass. These fiber-optic cables carry information in the form of light produced by a LASER. Even the tiniest fiber-optic cables can carry many more voice conversations simultaneously than a standard copper wire.

COAXIAL CABLE is used by many cable television companies. These companies take television programs broadcast from cities and from satellites and distribute the signals to neighborhood homes. J.H.

SEE ALSO: TELEVISION

Cacao see Cocoa

A large telephone cable carries many fine wires within it

Photo Courtesy of Western Electric

Cactus Cactus is the name for more than 1700 different plants. Some cacti are very large and tree-like. Other cacti are climbing vines. Still others look like tiny "balls." Most of these plants are alike because they have needle-like *spines* instead of leaves, soft-looking green bodies, and most live in hot dry places. Many cacti have large, pretty flowers which bloom in the spring. No cactus has blue flowers. While cacti grow in DESERTS all over the world today, they first grew only in the Americas.

Cactus flower   Saguaro, or giant cactus

All photos Courtesy Society For Visual Education, Inc.

Barrel cactus. These cactus plants can be found in deserts of the Southwest

Because the cactus lives in places where it very seldom rains, it stores great amounts of water in large cells in the center of the stem. The *barrel* cactus, which is common in the deserts of the United States, holds nine times its own weight in water. Many thirsty travelers drink from this cactus by cutting off the top, crushing the inside of the cactus between two stones, and then squeezing it in their hands. The *prickly pear* has a flat, fleshy, sectional stem on which yellow or reddish flowers bloom.

The cactus produces a juicy fruit inside of which are the seeds. The skin or peel of this fruit, like the green surface of the cactus itself, grows in such a way that it keeps the water inside. Instead of broad flat leaves such as other plants have, the cactus has hard narrow spines which do not dry out. The cactus is so completely fitted for living with very little water that too much rain can kill it.

While the body of the cactus, which is actually its *stem,* looks soft and fleshy, this is not usually the case. The *giant* cactus of the Southwest, 40 to 50 feet (12.19 to 15.24 meters) tall, has a material inside it that is so stiff that the Indians used to make carrying poles and frames for papoose cradles. They also used the hollowed out trunk of the barrel cactus as a cooking pot.

The spines of the cactus serve a double usefulness. Not only do they prevent evaporation, but they protect the cactus from animals which would otherwise eat it. The roots of most cacti branch widely so that when the rain does fall, they are able to absorb a great deal of it.

Thus, the cactus is well adapted to its life in arid climates. A shallow network of roots efficiently catches the rain which the central stem tissue stores for use in the dry season. Its protecting spines have no pores (stomata), and the stem has fewer stomata than other plants. Even those it does have are often set in depressions as a further safeguard against evaporation. The outer stem layer has a thick waxy coat (cutin) to prevent any water loss.   J. K. L.

SEE ALSO: LEAVES, STEM

Caddis fly (KAHD-ihss) Caddis flies are insects with slender bodies and hairy wing scales which make them look like MOTHS. They have aquatic LARVAE. The larvae spin silken webs and live in cases of sand and pebbles cemented together with strands of web.

SEE: INSECTA

Caddis fly; larva in case of small stones

Cadmium (CAD-mee-um) Cadmium is a silvery white metal closely related to ZINC in its properties and where it is found. It is never found uncombined in nature. Only one true cadmium mineral is known—*greenockite* (cadmium sulfide). This rare element with poisonous fumes is represented by the chemical symbol, Cd. It is obtained almost exclusively as a by-product of the smelting and refining of zinc ores.

Commercially, cadmium's greatest use is as a coating on iron and steel for protection from corrosion. It is much more practical and efficient than zinc for this purpose. Cadmium is also an ingredient in low-melting-point alloys, used in automatic devices. It melts at 320.9°C. (609.6°F). Cadmium has had atomic energy applications. The cadmium nucleus readily absorbs thermal neutrons. Cadmium alloy rods are used in nuclear reactors to absorb and control excess neutron production.

Cadmium was discovered in 1817 by Friedrich Strohmeyer of Germany. Its atomic number is 48. Its atomic weight is 112.40.   D.L.D.

Caffeine (kaff-EEN) Caffeine is a stimulant found in COFFEE, tea, and some soft drinks. It is derived from PURINE, a nitrogen compound.

Taken in moderation, such as by drinking one or two cups of coffee a day, caffeine seems to be harmless and may help people remain alert. There is increasing evidence, however, that too much caffeine can produce serious health problems and may be mildly addictive. Overuse of caffeine can cause sleeplessness and anxiety. It has also been linked to heart disease and other medical difficulties. Young people are most likely to get caffeine from soft drinks.   V.B.I./J.H.

Caisson (KAY-suhn) A caisson is a vertical chamber that is sunk deep below the surface to permit construction work to be performed. Often the work is done below the water level of rivers and harbors. In many caissons,

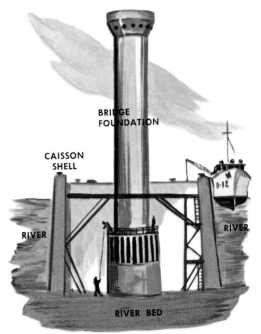

Caissons are used in building supports

men and machines prepare the space for foundations for buildings, BRIDGE abutments, piers, and tunnels.

Caissons can be made of wood, steel, or concrete. *Open caissons* are open at the top and bottom. *Box caissons* have a bottom but no top. *Pneumatic caissons* are airtight, and have a roofed chamber at the bottom where men work. Compressed air keeps the water out of the working chamber.

Workers called *sandhogs* descend into the caisson and dig out the soft mud and muck. This is raised through the shaft in buckets through *airlocks*. As the men work, the caisson sinks deeper by its own weight until it reaches a solid foundation. Wooden timbers or steel beams are often driven into the ground until they reach bedrock. The timbers or beams form a circle which is dug out and filled with concrete. These are used as a permanent foundation for the structure that is being built.

AIR COMPRESSORS work constantly to support the needed air pressure in a pneumatic caisson. As the caisson sinks deeper, the air pressure must be increased. Working under such pressures is dangerous. Construction companies follow strict precautions to keep their workers from developing the BENDS.
                                C.L.K./P.G.B.

Caisson disease see Bends

Calabash The calabash is a climbing herb with a weak stem. The herb sends out tendrils, which hang on to things. The fruit is a modified berry or pepo.

George J. Ball Inc.

Caladiums showing leaves of various colors

Caladium (kuh-LAY-dee-um) The caladium is a plant with leaves of many shapes and colors. They may be shaped like hearts or arrowheads, and may be green or mixtures of green, red, or yellow. The caladium is often grown as a house plant.

This plant is an annual with broad, palmately veined leaves. The FLOWER has five petals and a pistil of three united carpels. The FRUIT wall has a hard exocarp. The rest is fleshly. It is a Cucurbitaceae.

The caladium, like its close relative, TARO, rarely blossoms. Instead it spreads by means of a thick underground stem, called a TUBER. Caladium is the genus name commonly used but sometimes the plants are classified as *Colocasia*. The Colocasia originated in the tropics of Asia, while the caladium originated in tropical America. In either case, this tender PERENNIAL is an attractive addition to any garden.   J.K.L.

Calamine Calamine is an important ore of ZINC (zinc silicate) found in Europe and North America. It occurs in CRYSTALS. Calamine also refers to *zinc oxide* used in medicines and cosmetics.

Calcite see Rocks

Calcium (KAL-see-um) Calcium is a soft metal element which is silver-white in color. It is found in the earth's rocks, in green vegetables and fruits, and in milk. All plants and animals need calcium for their growth.

The diets of both adults and children must have large amounts of calcium compounds to develop strong teeth, sound bones, and healthy blood. Without calcium, the muscles of the body do not work properly, and bones and teeth weaken.

Calcium was discovered in 1808 by SIR HUMPHRY DAVY. Its atomic number is 20, atomic weight 40.08, symbol, Ca. It is rarely found free in nature because it combines actively with water.

Two important calcium compounds are GYPSUM—used to make plaster of Paris—and lime (calcium oxide) from $CaCO_3$.

Pure calcium metal is prepared by melting the oxide or carbonate in an electric furnace.

When placed in water, calcium metal reacts vigorously to produce calcium hydroxide and free hydrogen gas, along with much heat. Lime, calcium oxide, also reacts vigorously with water to form calcium hydroxide.

SEE ALSO: ELEMENTS IN THE HUMAN BODY

Calcium carbonate (KAL-see-um CAR-bun-ate) Calcium carbonate is one of the most common MINERALS in the earth's crust. It is found in the impure form of marble, limestone, chalk, seashells, coral, egg shells, and is responsible for cave formations.

Pure calcium carbonate, which has a chemical formula of $CaCO_3$, exists in two crystalline forms—*aragonite* and *calcite*. Aragonite is the less stable form, but at lower temperatures and higher pressures it becomes stable. CALCITE is found in the form of pure limestone, white marble, or in transparent crystals, sometimes called *iceland spar*.

Calcium carbonate is used in the manufacture of paint, rubber, dentifrices, paper and chalk.   D. L. D.

SEE ALSO: ROCKS, STALACTITE, STALAGMITE

Calculator A calculator is an instrument used for computations. The addition, subtraction, multiplication, or division problem is entered on a keyboard. The calculator does the computation, and the result is shown on the display. The electronic calculator often performs computations with great speed.

Texas Instruments

Some calculators produce printouts.

Calculators vary in the functions they perform and how they perform. They may have keys to find percentages, powers, square roots, etc. Some calculators are programmable; that is, users can set up a special routine and activate it by one key. Others provide printouts instead of just displaying the final result.   M.M.L.

SEE ALSO: ADDING MACHINE, COMPUTER

Calculus see Mathematics

Calendar A calendar is a record of the time it takes the earth to make one revolution around the sun. Today most of the countries of the world use a calendar which has 365 days in each year.

A year is the period of time it takes the earth to make one orbit around the sun. Since the earth's year is a little longer than 365 days, one day is added to the calendar every fourth year to make *leap year.*

A perfect calendar would be so set that the earth arrived at the same point in its orbit at precisely the same time and date each year. Since the earth's rotation does not fit into the period of revolution exactly, a perfect calendar seems almost impossible. The length of a year is about 365 days, 5 hours, 48 minutes, and 46 seconds, slightly less than 365¼ days.

Since the days of early Roman Empire, man has devised many different calendars. Among these have been the *Roman* and *Julian* calendars. The calendar in use by most countries today is the *Gregorian* calendar, developed by Pope Gregory XIII. On this calendar, the length of the year is shortened slightly by omitting three days every 400 years. Ordinarily every year divisible by four is a leap year. On the Gregorian cal-

endar, a *century year* is not a leap year unless its first two numbers are divisible by four. As an example, in any four successive centurial years, only one can be a leap year. This eliminates three days in each 400-year period, making the Gregorian calendar nearly perfect. The Gregorian calendar was also known as the New Style calendar.

There have been many different proposals for a new worldwide calendar. A United Nations committee was formed to study the problem. They proposed a new world calendar. The committee's proposal, however, was not adopted.   H. S. G.

Calendula (kuh-LENN-juh-luh) Calendula are a group of flowers which have large blossoms made of many yellow or orange petals. These blossoms can be used to flavor soups or stews. The most common calendula is the MARIGOLD.   J.K.L.

Californium (cal-ih-FOR-nee-um) Californium, ELEMENT 98, is manmade and RADIOACTIVE. It is an ACTINIDE ELEMENT. S.G. Thompson, K. Street, Jr., A. Ghierse, and G.T. Seaborg discovered the ISOTOPE $^{245}_{98}$Cf in 1950. Californium may be formed in stellar explosions such as supernovas. The half life of Californium-254 is 55 days. This information agrees with the light produced by these explosions.

Californium has 12 isotopes. Atomic mass numbers vary from 242 through 254. Although rare, it has now been made in gram amounts. *Oxidation number* or VALENCE is + 3. HALF-LIFE ranges from 3.7 minutes to 892 years. These half-lives were found by new methods of *mass spectrometry,* using such tiny amounts as 4 nanograms (four billionths of a gram). $^{252}_{98}$Cf, half-life 2.65 years, upon spontaneous fission yields

2,400,000,000 neutrons per *milligram.* Thus, $^{252}_{98}Cf$ can be used as a source of neutrons and to study nuclear fission. Californium was first prepared at the University of California (Berkeley) by bombardment in their 60-inch (152.4 centimeter) CYCLOTRON. The new element was named for the state and the university.

M.S.P./A.J.H.

SEE ALSO: ATOM, MENDELEEV'S PERIODIC TABLE, NUCLEAR SCIENCE.

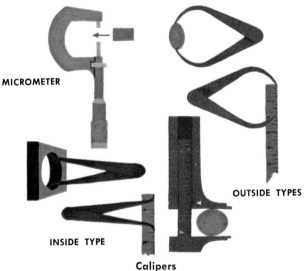

MICROMETER

INSIDE TYPE

OUTSIDE TYPES

Calipers

Caliper (KAL-ih-per) A caliper is used to find the size of an object that cannot be measured with a straight line rule. Two arms are set to the size of an object and then compared to a ruler.

An outside caliper can measure diameters and thicknesses of tree trunks, balls, rods, bars, etc. The size of an opening in an object can be measured with calipers whose arms touch inside surfaces.

Some calipers have a scale which shows the measurement directly when the caliper arms touch an object's surface. Measurements of fine machine parts are taken with a screw micrometer caliper. F.R.W.

SEE ALSO: MEASUREMENT

Calm, regions of Regions of calm are places in the ATMOSPHERE where there is no horizontal air motion or wind. They are the opposite of the JET STREAMS.

Calorie The calorie is a unit for measuring HEAT energy. It is used to describe the necessary heat needed to raise the temperature of water a desired amount. In food chemistry, it refers to the heat energy which a particular food can yield.

More precisely, one calorie of heat applied to one gram of water raises its temperature one degree Centigrade. Water requires more heat to raise its temperature one degree than does the same amount of other common substances. For example, one gram of copper takes only one-eleventh calorie to rise one degree Centigrade. One gram of aluminum takes about one-fifth calorie. The large Calorie (with a capital "C") is 1000 small calories.

The gram-calorie is a very small unit of heat energy. One gram is only one-four hundred fifty-fourth ($\frac{1}{454}$) of a pound. Because the calorie is so small, food chemists use the large Calorie to measure the energy in foods.

One large Calorie (or kilogram-calorie) of heat applied to 1,000 grams (about 2.2 pounds) of water raises its temperature one degree Centigrade. A slice of bread containing 100 Calories actually equals 100,000 small calories. J. H. D.

SEE ALSO: BRITISH THERMAL UNIT, CALORIMETRY

Calorimetry (kal-uh-RIMM-uh-tree) Calorimetry refers to the measurement of the quantity of heat exchanged by a test body with the apparatus called the calorimeter. The measurement of heat ENERGY is carried out in a *calorimeter.* One kind of calorimeter has two metal cans; one small can is placed inside a larger can. The small can is held in place with a large fiber washer. An air space exists between the containers. A wooden lid is provided with a hole for inserting a stirring rod and another for a thermometer. The air space between the walls helps reduce the loss or gain of heat from the surroundings.

If a definite weight of cool water is placed inside the calorimeter and its temperature measured, and some heated material added, it is possible to find out how much heat is received by the cold water. The number of calories of heat received by the water and the container holding it may be calculated.

The functioning of a calorimeter is based on the Law of Conservation of Energy. The heat lost by a warm body equals the heat gained by the cooler body which receives it.

One CALORIE of heat applied to one gram of water raises its temperature one degree C. Only a fraction of a calorie is required to raise the temperature of one gram of most common materials one degree C. This quantity of heat is called the *specific heat* of a substance. To find the total calories of heat energy needed to raise the temperature of any mass any number of degrees, multiply the mass, in grams, by the specific heat by the change in temperature, in degrees C.

The calorimeter provides a way to measure the specific heat of various materials. It may be used also to find the heat required to melt a gram of ice.

Special types of calorimeters are used to measure the heat values of fuels or foods. Often a *bomb calorimeter* is used. The fuel (or food) with a supply of oxygen is burned in an enclosed metal container surrounded by water. The heat given off is received by the water. From the rise in temperature of the water, the heat value of the fuel in calories may be calculated. Foods are handled in the same way, but they are expressed in kilogram-calories, which are 1,000 times larger than gram-calories.   J. H. D.
SEE ALSO: HEAT OF FUSION, HEAT OF VAPORIZATION

Calyx (KAY-lix) The calyx is the part of a FLOWER which protects the BUD. It is divided into leaf-shaped *sepals* below the petals. After the flower opens, the calyx may fall off. More often, however, it forms a little cup around the petals. Sometimes the calyx remains after the petals of the flower have dropped off.

The calyx may have separate parts, called *sepals,* or it may be one continuous piece. The SEPALS are rarely stalked. When the sepals match the petals, an inexperienced observer often thinks that the flower has no calyx. Actually only a few kinds of flowering plants lack them.   J. K. L.
SEE ALSO: ANGIOSPERMS, PETAL

Cambium (KAM-bee-um) Cambium is that part of the plant which helps it to grow in width. Plants have only four areas of cells with the power to divide and increase the size of the plant. The stem tip and root tip help the plant to grow taller and the roots to extend deeper into the soil.

The growth of a plant in width, or circumference, is accomplished by two kinds of tissue with the ability to multiply—the cork cambium and the vascular cambium.

The vascular cambium separates the PHLOEM from the XYLEM cells. When bark is peeled from a trunk of a tree the cambial layer is exposed. This cambium makes new xylem and phloem cells throughout the growing season.

Cork cambium is found between the cork and phloem in the bark of trees. It produces cork cells which protect the plant from internal loss of water and external attack by insects and other enemies. Without cambial tissue all plants would live one year and die. All secondary growth of BIENNIALS and PERENNIALS is produced by the cambium and plant tips.   H. J. C.
SEE ALSO: ANNUAL RINGS

Camel Camels are large animals with humps on their backs. One kind of camel has one hump. Another kind has two humps. Camels have long legs, long curved necks, small heads, and heavy bodies. Camels are used to carry riders or heavy loads.

The camels with one hump are the *Arabian camels,* or *dromedaries.* They live in the hot desert countries of Arabia, Asia and North Africa. They are sleeker and longer legged than the *Bactrian* or *two-humped* camels and are especially good for riding. With a rider they can run at a rate of about 8-10 miles (12.87-16.09 kilometers) an hour and can travel about 100 miles (160

Patrick Cavanaugh

Bactrian camel

Courtesy Society For Visual Education, Inc.

Arabian or dromedary camel

kilometers) a day. Riding a camel is different from riding a horse. The camel moves both right legs together and then both left legs. The effect is a rolling, swaying motion. The camel is 7 to 8 feet (2.13 to 2.44 meters) tall. Before a rider can mount he must make the camel kneel down. Camels have hard pads on their knees and chests.

The camel's feet have two toes. Arabian camels have soft cushions on their wide feet so that they do not sink into the sand. The soft, woolly hair of the Arabian camel is especially fine. It is yellow-brown and gets darker as the camel gets older.

Two-humped or Bactrian camels live in Central Asia from China to Iran. They are adapted to life in colder climates and on rocky or mountainous land. Bactrian camels have shorter legs than dromedaries. The soles of their feet are harder. They grow long, shaggy winter coats which are shed in spring. Bactrian camels are mainly pack animals. With a load of 400 to 500 pounds (181 to 227 kilograms), they can travel at a rate of 2 or 3 miles (3.22 or 4.83 kilometers) an hour and can go 30 miles (48.28 kilometers) in one day.

Camels are not as intelligent as horses or elephants. But the camel's needs are few and well adapted to its desert habitat. In a sandstorm, its slit-like nostrils and its long eyelids with their double rows of lashes close against the blowing sands.

Camels have the ability to go without water until 25% of their body weight is lost. This may take up to eight days. Camels do not gain water by stomach storage nor by use of fat in the hump. At night their temperature drops to about 93° F. (34° C.). During the day it slowly rises to 105° F. (41° C.) before the camel begins to sweat freely. Also, camel wool insulates. The camel never sheds hair on the dorsal surface. Since fat stores are in the hump, fat insulation on the rest of the body does not pre-vent outward flow of heat. Tissues suffer from water loss but blood fluidity remains almost normal. Kidney excretion is reduced. All of these methods conserve water.

Camels are vegetarians and are satisfied with almost any kind of herbaceous plants or grasses. They have stiff, hard lips to break off the skimpy foliage they find in desert or rocky country.

Camels have been domesticated for thousands of years. They give an appearance of docility and gentleness but they are rarely affectionate. They remember mistreatments and hold grudges, spitting at their offenders or biting them.   C.L.K.

Camellia (kuh-MEEL-yuh) The camellia is an evergreen tree or bush. Its lovely flowers are often worn as corsages. The pink, red, or white flowers are waxy and the leaves are a shiny, dark green.

The camellia is native to Asia and belongs to the tea *(Thaceae)* family. In the North, camellias are grown in cool greenhouses, but in the South they grow outdoors in moist shady spots, where they blossom in the winter and spring. PROPAGATION is by cuttings.

The dried leaves of *Camellia sasanqua* have a pleasant taste and are often mixed with tea leaves. The oil from *Camellia drupifera* is used in medicine. *Camellia japonica* and *Camellia creticulata* are odorless and are the kinds most commonly grown for their blossoms.   J. M. C.

Camellia

MAKING A CAMERA THAT WORKS

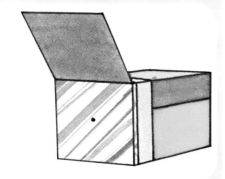

Material: film box, foil, photographic
film (Kodak Tri-X), devel-
oper, rinse, fixer, black
paint.

1 A homemade camera which will take
   pictures on film may be constructed.
   This project should be done with
   someone familiar with film process-
   ing.
2 Tape a piece of foil on one end of the
   film box.
3 Use a small needle to make a small
   hole in the center of the foil.
4 Paint the inside of the box with black
   paint.
5 In a dark room tape a piece of film to
   the other end of the box. Close the end
   of the box and lower the front flap.
6 Aim your camera at some object and
   lift the flap for one or two seconds.
   Then carefully lower the flap. Do not
   move the camera while the flap is up.
7 Develop your film.

Camera A camera is a small box free
of light inside. When a picture is
taken, light enters through a hole and
falls on the uncovered film inside. The
film is treated with three chemical
solutions to make a negative. The
negative is used to make the photograph.

  When using a camera, some of the light
reflecting from the subject enters through
the hole, or aperture, and is focused by the
lens system, producing an image on the
emulsion side of the film. The shutter controls the length of time the light falls on the
film.

  The simplest camera is a *box camera.* The
shutter speed is unchangeable, so its use is
limited to well-lighted, still subjects. Since it
has a fixed focus, the distance from the
camera to the subject must be a certain
number of feet or meters. This camera's
aperture size cannot be changed.

  Most other cameras have variable shutter
speed, aperture, and focus. The *110-car-
tridge camera* is small and easily carried. The
126-cartridge camera is very easy to use and
gives a larger negative than the 110 camera.
The *35mm viewfinder cameras* are usually
very light and of very high quality. The
35mm single lens reflex camera allows the
photographer to see what is recorded on the
film. The single lens reflex comes with
interchangeable lenses and a "through-the-

HOW DOES A CAMERA WORK?

Material: cracker box, tissue paper,
candle

1 Cover an open end of a cracker box
   with white tissue paper. Tape it se-
   curely in place to avoid wrinkles in
   the paper. Make a pin hole in the
   center of the closed end of the box.
2 Take the "camera" into a dark room.
   Set a lighted candle two feet in front
   of the pinhole. Stand behind the
   "camera" and observe the pattern on
   the tissue paper.
3 Since light travels in straight lines
   the top of the flame will show on the
   bottom of the picture on the tissue
   paper. The image is upside down.

American Broadcasting Corp.

TV cameras provide on-the-spot coverage of major events.

lens" metering system. These are the best of the 35mm cameras. The *double lens reflex camera* uses a large film size, which gives a better enlarged print. It also allows the photographer to see what the film sees. The *large format cameras* are single lens reflex cameras, which use larger sized films. A very late development in small cameras is the disk camera, which uses film in a compact round disk rather than a long roll.

Self-printing cameras use films that contain the chemicals needed to finish the photograph. There are many films used in the self-printing cameras: black and white print; black and white negative; color print, that needs to be timed; and color films that develop themselves. Self-printing cameras also produce colored motion pictures.

The *movie camera* takes many pictures per second with a stop-and-go advance film mechanism. Movie cameras come with many features. It is possible to vary the number of pictures per second. This allows the photographer to produce slow motion studies. Movie cameras have automatic lenses that correct the exposures of the film for differing amounts of light. Movie cameras have zoom lenses that produce wide angle or telephoto scenes from the same camera. Sound movie cameras record on magnetic tape the sounds related to the action recorded by the film.

The *television camera* has only its lens in common with the photo camera. Television usually uses a zoom lens. After the light enters the TV camera it falls on a photoelectric element which converts the light image to an electric signal. This signal can be recorded on magnetic tape or it can be transmitted "live" to TV sets. Magnetic tape can be stored or used to give viewers an instant replay of the action.

Major camera parts are the *lens, diaphragm,* and *shutter.* The quality of the lens determines the quality of the picture and the size of the image on the film. The diaphragm controls the amount of light that enters the camera and the area in front of the camera that is in focus. The shutter also controls the light that hits the film.

A.J.H./M.W.K.

SEE ALSO: LENS, MAN-MADE; MOTION PICTURES; PHOTOGRAPHY; TELEVISION

Camomile Camomile is a PERENNIAL plant of the THISTLE family. The dried flowers are used in home remedies.

Courtesy Society For Visual Education, Inc.

The whippoorwill (above) and the American lizard (below) use camouflage to blend with their surroundings.

Courtesy Society For Visual Education, Inc.

Camouflage (KAMM-uh-flahzh) Camouflage means to hide an object or to confuse an enemy as to the object's presence, location, or characteristics. Camouflage, which takes advantage of natural means of concealment, or provides artificial ones, is based on PROTECTIVE COLORATION — a principle found in the animal world. The zebra's pattern makes it less visible in its natural surroundings, as does the white color of the polar bear against an ice background. The CHAMELEON'S ability to change color is another example.   D.L.D.

Camphor (KAMM-fer) Camphor is a whitish compound from the camphor tree—native to China, Japan and Formosa. Camphor is obtained by DISTILLATION of the finely-ground wood and leaves. It is then refined down to commercial gum camphor. It has a penetrating, characteristic odor and a pungent, aromatic taste.

Camphor is used medicinally as a liniment, analgesic, and as a gastrointestinal drug. It is important in the manufacture of celluloid and nitrocellulose compounds, in perfumes, photographic film, insect repellent, and as a retardant for tarnish on silver and mildew on wood.   D. L. D.

Canal A canal is a man-made waterway used for shipping or for irrigating land. Ship canals are built for three main reasons. A canal may connect two big bodies of water. A canal may be built around a section of a river with falls or rapids. A canal may provide a waterway to a city which has no outlet to a river or a sea.

The Egyptians built a canal in 2000 B.C., joining the Nile River and the Red Sea. One of the longest and oldest canals was begun around 500 B.C. in China. The Erie Canal (1825) was the first significant canal in the United States. It connected Lake Erie and the Hudson River and was important in the westward development of the country.

Usually, canals are built wide enough to allow two ships to pass each other, and are deep enough to retain a 1½ foot (.46 meter) margin of water beneath the largest of ships.

A simple lock-type canal

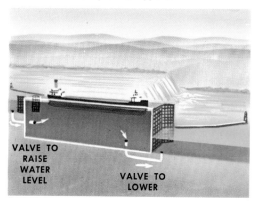

VALVE TO
RAISE
WATER
LEVEL   VALVE TO
                  LOWER

A *lock,* first used by the Dutch in the 14th century, is a water elevator. A watertight gate is located at each end of the lock. The gates close after a boat enters the lock. The ship is then moved up or down by adjusting the water level. Important canals are the Panama Canal, the Suez Canal, and the canals in the St. Lawrence Seaway. P. F. D.

Male (left) and female canaries

Canary Canaries are finches. They belong to the same family as buntings, cardinals, and grosbeaks. Goldfinches are wild canaries. Several species are found throughout America. Most of them are various combinations of yellow and black.

The common American goldfinch has a yellow body with black wings and crown. Their swooping flight reminds one of a roller coaster. Breeding occurs in late summer when thistles are in bloom. Nests are lined with thistledown and built in trees or hedges. Four to six pale blue eggs are laid. They hatch in about two weeks.

Domestic canaries come from Old World species around the Canary Islands. J. C. K.

Cancer (constellation) Cancer is a group of stars which has been imagined to look like a crab. This CONSTELLATION can be seen in the spring. Cancer is one of the signs of the ZODIAC.

The sun reaches the sign of Cancer about June 21st. At this time the sun can be seen directly overhead at noon at an imaginary line called the *Tropic of Cancer.* This line marks the most northern limit of the places on Earth where the sun can be seen directly overhead at noon.

On a very clear evening the constellation Cancer looks like a silvery cloud between two faint stars. When a telescope is used to look at the cloud it can be seen to be a

Cancer, the Crab

cluster of faint stars. It is sometimes called *Praesepe,* or the *Manger.* The two stars beside it are called *Aselli,* the donkeys who are eating out of the Manger. Sometimes the cluster is called the *Beehive.* The star cluster of Cancer has long been a weather signal. When it can be seen, fair weather is ahead. It is held that before a storm, the Manger cannot be seen at all.

The Greeks believed that this star pattern was a memorial to the crab which Juno had sent to bite Hercules when he was fighting with the monster Hydra.   C. L. K.

Cancer (disease) Cancer is a growth of cells which form *malignant* tumors. Unless something is done to stop the cell growth, cancer may take a person's life. A malignant tumor is in contrast to a *benign* tumor. A benign tumor grows more slowly. It will not take a person's life, but it may cause sickness and pain when it grows, because of the pressure on other organs.

The basic cellular structure of a cancer is the *epithelial* cell, one of the many kinds of cells which make up the body. It is an epithelial cell gone wrong—one that does not live by the rules which govern all other cells. The epithelial cells are the kind which make up the skin. They line all canals of the body to which air has access and organs having a very special kind of work to do, such as the liver and kidneys.

Cancer cells endanger life in two different ways. One threat is called *invasiveness.* When a benign tumor grows, it may push against other organs, causing discomfort and possibly other problems. Cells in a malignant tumor, how-

ever, have a tendency to grow directly into nearby organs. When too many normal cells are replaced by cancerous cells, the organ will not be able to operate properly or at all.

The second threat is called *metastasis.* Cancer cells often break away from a tumor and travel through the bloodstream to other parts of the body. When they lodge and begin to reproduce, more malignant tumors may begin to grow. In general, cancer treatment is far more effective if it begins before the stage of metastasis is reached. Cells from benign tumors do not metastasize.

The CHROMOSOMES in cells making up malignant tumors are usually structured abnormally. As the cells reproduce, the abnormalities are passed on. Studies from the 1980s and 1990s increasingly suggest that at least some types of cancer may be linked to HEREDITY. In 1991, a single defective gene was identified that seemed to trigger colon cancer. About one out of every five thousand people inherit the gene.

Traditionally, scientists have believed that the majority of cancers are caused by overexposure to such things as cigarette smoke and other airborne pollutants, certain chemicals, alcohol, and certain types of RADIATION (including sunlight). Anything that can produce cancer is called a CARCINOGEN. By the 1990s, evidence was mounting that heredity may help determine people's susceptibility to at least some carcinogens.

Malignant tumors can grow in many places, but frequently begin in the skin, lungs, breasts, prostate glands, and colon. LEUKEMIA is cancer of the blood. It often strikes children.

All cancer treatment involves killing cancerous cells while trying to limit damage to healthy cells. Early detection greatly improves the patient's chances of survival. Techniques to destroy cancer cells include surgical removal, bombardment with X rays, and the use of drugs. Using drugs to combat cancer is called CHEMOTHERAPY.   J.H./E.S.S.

SEE ALSO: ASBESTOS; RADIATION, BIOLOGICAL EFFECTS; RADIATION, USES; TUMORS

Normal cell structure (below left) is enlarged 175 times. The tissue (E) is the epithelium that lines the respiratory tract. An early cancerous condition (below right) is enlarged 65 times.

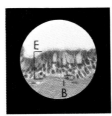

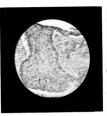

National Teaching Aids, Inc.

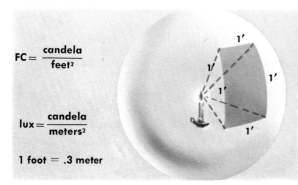

$$FC = \frac{candela}{feet^2}$$

$$lux = \frac{candela}{meters^2}$$

1 foot = .3 meter

The sphere represents a transparent ball which has a radius of one foot. A light source of one candela is placed at the exact center. When a one-foot square is drawn on the surface of the sphere, and lines are drawn from the corners of this to the light source, a solid angle, or *steradian*, is formed. The intensity of light emitted through this angle is one *lumen*, and the amount of light falling on the surface of the sphere is one candela

Candela (*Candlepower*) Candela is the new unit for measuring the visible LIGHT energy per unit area coming from a glowing body. It replaces the terms *candle* and *candlepower*. We call the light energy per unit area the *luminous intensity*. One candela is the light emitted from 1/60th of a square *centimeter* of surface of *incandescent* platinum at 2046° Kelvin, the freezing point of platinum.

The terms *luminous intensity* (unit: candela), *luminous flux* (unit: *lumen*), and IL-LUMINATION (metric unit: *lux;* English unit: *foot-candle*) are easily confused. To understand light units, one must first analyze light as RADIANT ENERGY.

Each glowing body gives off *radiant energy* in *all* directions. This radiant energy is composed of visible (light) energy and invisible (ELECTROMAGNETIC) energy. The light energy emitted is luminous energy.

Luminous flux represents the total amount of light from a glowing body per unit *time*. The unit of luminous flux, English system or metric, is the *lumen,* the amount of light from a one candela strength source striking a one square unit spherical surface one unit of length from the candela. These measurements define a solid angle called a *steradian*. It is this angle which is important here and not the units in feet, meters, square feet or square meters. Thus, in the metric system, the lumen is the light striking a surface one meter square and one meter distant from a one candela source. The illustration shows the English system. The lumen is the unit in both.

Illumination is the light received by any object some distance from the glowing body emitting that light. Its formula is illumination equals candela divided by distance squared. Its units are *lux* and footcandle. Measurements of illumination are made by *photoelectric* cells.   M. S. P.

SEE ALSO: INVERSE SQUARE LAW, LIGHT, PHOTOMETER

Evergreen candytuft

Candytuft The candytuft has a wide flat blossom made up of many small, four-petaled flowers. These plants first came from the countries along the Mediterranean Sea. The flowers are white, red, or purple, and some have a very pleasant smell. The common candytuft, about 10 inches (25.4 centimeters) tall, is often grown as a garden border.

All candytufts have the shorter stemmed flowers in the center of the blossom. The two outer petals of the flower are longer than the inner. The sap has a strong odor, and the whole plant feels soft and downy. Some candytufts are shrubs, others are evergreens or PERENNIALS, but the common varieties are ANNUALS.   J. K. L.

Cane see Grasses, Palm

Cane sugar see Sugar

Canis Major and Canis Minor
(KAY-niss) Canis Major and Canis
Minor are two groups of stars that
have been imagined to represent dogs.
Canis Major means the *Greater Dog*.
Canis Minor means the *Lesser Dog*.
They are not very large CONSTELLA-
TIONS, but each of them has one very
bright star. Canis Major contains the
brightest star in the sky, SIRIUS. These
two constellations can be seen in the
wintertime, near the famous hunter
constellation ORION.

The stars of Canis Major are usually
pictured as a dog standing on its hind legs.
Sirius is either the dog's nose or his jaw.
Canis Minor has fewer stars. Its bright star,
PROCYON, is the dog's body and three smaller
stars form the curve of its head. Sirius,
Procyon, and BETELGEUSE, the bright star in
Orion, form an equilateral triangle some-
times called the *Winter Triangle*.

The most famous explanation of these
star dogs is that they belong to the hunter,
ORION. Other stories say that Canis Major
is a memorial to a very fast dog, Laelops,
who ran a race with a fox. Another story
is that they are the goddess Diana's hunting
dogs.

In ancient times Sirius was in the sky during the day in the summertime. It was
invisible, but the people believed that Sirius
combined its heat with the sun's heat to
make midsummer almost unbearable. They
called this period "dog days." C.L.K.

Canker worm Canker worms, also
called *measuring* WORMS, are MOTH larvae. They destroy leaves.

Canker sore Canker sores, painful
white spots on the mouth's lining, are
caused by certain fungi or bacteria.
Occasionally, cold sores (caused by a
virus) are mistakenly called canker
sores.

Canker sores (properly called aphthous
ulcers) sometimes occur when a person has
taken an antibiotic for a long time. This
allows resistant bacteria or yeasts to take
over in the mouth, causing infection or
pain. Sometimes a tooth will snag and open
a spot for infection to get in. The best treatment is cleanliness of the mouth and
specific medications applied to the sore
areas. E.S.S.

Canna see Plants, tropical

Canned heat Canned heat is a gel
form of alcohol used to heat small
quantities of water or food.

Canned heat, or solid alcohol, is a combination of methyl alcohol or denatured
ethyl alcohol and a second ingredient. The
second ingredient may be cellulose acetate,
cellulose nitrate, or calcium acetate.

Canned heat can be made by combining a
saturated solution of calcium acetate with
either methyl or ethyl alcohol in a one-to-
six ratio. This semi-solid gel burns with a
blue flame characteristic of burning alcohol.
A.J.H.

Cannibal fish see Tropical fish

Canning see Food preservation

Cannon see Weapons

Cantaloupe see Melons

Cantilever see Bridges

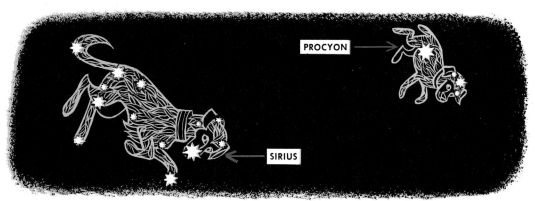

Canis Major, the Big Dog, and Canis Minor, the Little Dog, have major stars included in their figures

Canyon A canyon is a deep cut in the earth's surface. Its very steep sides have been carved into the crust of the earth by running water or by the action of glacial ice. Canyons are found on the ocean floor as well as on the continents. Ocean canyons, called *trenches,* are often very deep.

Most canyons found on the continents are formed in mountainous regions that have high plateaus. Some canyons are hundreds of feet deep, but the bottom of a canyon is never found to be below sea level. Once sea level is reached, the cutting action of running water stops. When this happens, the river that has created the canyon is said to be in the stage of old age.

In the United States, the Grand Canyon in Arizona is the largest and probably the best known. It has been cut through the many layers of stratified sedimentary rock that make up the *Colorado Plateau.* These exposed layers of sedimentary rock reveal the geologic history of that region that covers a vast period of time. The layers of different colored rocks are an awesome sight. H. S. G.

SEE ALSO: GEOLOGY

Capacitor see Condenser

Cape A piece of land that extends or juts out into an ocean or a lake is called a *cape.* Some of the more well-known capes are Cape of Good Hope, Cape Cod, and Cape Horn.

Cape Canaveral Cape Canaveral is 15,000 acres (6,070 hectares) of land on Florida's east coast. From late 1963 to April 1, 1974, it was known as Cape Kennedy. The Cape has been the Air Force Missile Test Center since 1950. Missiles for all military services are tested here and research satellites and space probes launched here. The test range extends from the Cape, about 6,000 miles (9,656 kilometers) south into the Atlantic Ocean.

SEE ALSO: ASTRONAUTICS, SPACE TRAVEL

Capella see Auriga

Caper (KAY-puhr) Capers are the flower buds of a Mediterranean white flowering shrub. The bud is picked and pickled for use in salads and meat sauces.

Capillarity (kapp-uh-LAIR-uh-tee) When the surface of a liquid is "free," as in a large bowl of water or bath tub, it is considered to be flat or horizontal except where the water comes into contact with the sides of the container. Here, the surface of the liquid may be curved up or down. The amount and direction of curvature depends on the type of liquid and the material from which the container is made. This curvature of the liquid surface results in capillary action.

Water, in contact with a vertical surface of glass, is curved upward because the molecules of glass exert forces on the molecules of liquid. These forces are called forces of *adhesion.* The force exerted by one molecule of liquid on another liquid molecule are called forces of *cohesion.* Molecules of mercury have a strong cohesive tendency and under the above conditions the surface of mercury will be curved downward against the vertical surface of glass. The angle that the liquid makes with the solid surface is called the angle of contact.

When a glass tube with a very small hole (called a *capillary tube*), open at both ends, is placed vertically in a container filled with water, the water in the tube tends to rise above the level of the liquid in the container. However, if a glass tube of the same bore is placed in a container of mercury, the mercury in the tube will be at a level which is lower than that of the mercury in the container. This is because the surface of the water curves upward where it contacts the glass, thus tending to pull more water up into the tube. Since the surface of the mercury curves downward where it contacts the glass, it tends to push the mercury out of the tube.

The amount of CAPILLARY rise depends on the diameter of the tube and on the surface tension and density of the liquid.

SEE ALSO: SURFACE TENSION

✳ THINGS TO DO

EXPERIMENTING WITH ADHESION AND COHESION TO SHOW CAPILLARITY

1″ = 2.5 cm.

1   Put an inch of water in a milk bottle. Place one end of a strip of blotting paper in the water with the other end hanging out of the mouth of the bottle. Notice the movement of water up the blotter.

2   Set a cube of sugar in a saucer containing a film of ink solution. Can you see the ink go up the sugar?

3   Place one end of a lamp wick in a glass of water. Let the other end hang out. Put a pan under this end to catch the water as it comes up the wick and drips off the exposed end.

4   Set the ends of several glass tubes with varying widths in a colored solution. Observe the water rise.

5   Place a stalk of fresh celery in a glass of red dye. After one hour cut a cross-section of the celery and notice the red circles.

6   Explanation: Water molecules adhere to the molecules of the material above it—the blotter, glass tube, sugar, lamp wick, and celery. This pull is greater than the cohesion or sticking together of one water molecule to the adjoining water molecule.

Capillary (KAP-puh-lair-ee) Capillaries are the smallest blood vessels circulating blood throughout the body. The two main types of blood vessels are arteries and veins. Arteries are largest when they leave the heart. Farther from the heart they become smaller. The smallest arteries are called *arterioles*. Arterioles grade into capillaries, and from the capillaries veins arise. These veins become larger as they near the heart. The smallest of the veins are known as *venules*.

Capillaries have thin walls one cell thick, supported by delicate connective tissue sheaths. They branch and rebranch among tissue cells. Blood plasma, minus blood cells and large protein molecules, diffuses out of the capillaries and becomes tissue fluid. It carries digested food and oxygen to surrounding tissue cells. Cells discharge their metabolic wastes and carbon dioxide into the tissue fluid. Blood pressure prevents return of the fluid to capillaries. The waste-laden fluid enters lymph vessels. It is finally returned to the blood by veins in the arms (*subclavians*). Shortly before these enter the large veins to the heart, right and left lymphatic ducts open into them.

Usually capillaries connect veins to arteries. In a few places as in fingers, toes, and lips, venules and arterioles join directly without capillary connection. This type of union is believed to play a role in heat regulation.

In organs like the liver, *sinusoids* take the place of capillaries. Their walls are irregular, formed by *engulfing cells* (phagocytes) and non-phagocytic cells. Phagocytes project into the lumen of the sinusoids.   J. C. K.

SEE ALSO: ARTERY, LYMPHATIC DUCT, LYMPHATIC SYSTEM, VEIN

TODAY'S HEALTH, published by AMERICAN MEDICAL ASSOCIATION

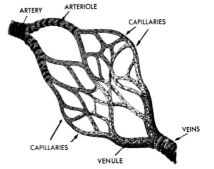

Capricornus, the Goat

Capricornus (kapp-ruh-KOR-nus) Capricornus is the CONSTELLATION that is sometimes called the *Goat,* or the *Sea Goat.* This group of stars looks like a bent triangle. It is a rather faint, autumn constellation and is one of the signs of the ZODIAC.

When the sun is in the sign of Capricorn, in December, it is highest overhead in the southern part of the world. The imaginary line that marks the southern boundary of the path of the sun is called the "Tropic of Capricorn."

According to one legend, the goat represents the god Bacchus, who assumed the shape of a goat one day to escape a giant named Typhon. Some ancient star maps picture Capricornus as a Sea Goat, or a creature with the head of a goat and the tail of a fish. This figure was supposed to represent the god Pan, who assumed this shape one day as he was frolicking in the Nile. Some stories mix the two legends and say that the sea goat was the shape that Pan took to escape from Typhon.   C. L. K.

Capsicum see Cayenne

Capsule (CAP-suhl) A capsule is a seed-pod that is divided into sections or compartments. When the SEEDS are ripe, the dry capsule opens so that the seeds may be shaken out.

Capsules are not all alike. The plantain capsule, for example, opens around the top, which comes off like a lid. The poppy capsule has many sections, each with a small hole at the top covered by a valve, and each containing many seeds.

A capsule is the fruit of a flower with a compound ovary.   J. M. C.

SEE ALSO: ANGIOSPERMS, FRUIT, PLANT

Capybara The capybara is a large South American rodent. It looks like a GUINEA PIG but may weigh as much as 100 pounds (45.36 kilograms.) It lives along river banks and lake shores.

SEE: RODENTIA

Carat In 1907, the carat began to be used by gem cutters as a unit of measure. It is also used to show that amount of pure GOLD in a mixture made of gold and other materials.

As a unit of weight for precious stones, the carat has been standardized by the United States government at 200 milligrams (1/5 gram, 3.08647 grains in English measurement). A two-carat diamond thus weighs 400 milligrams or 2/5 of one gram. This weight, 200 milligrams, has been accepted by most leading governments of the world. In the other meaning of the word, the *gold carat,* sometimes spelled *karat,* stood for a 24th part of the weight of the gold marc. It now means just a 24th part and is used to state the *proportion* of gold in an alloy. Thus 14-carat gold contains 14/24ths of gold mixed with 10/24ths of some other metal, usually silver or copper.

The word *carat* originally came from a Greek word that referred to locust seeds, each weighing about 205 milligrams.   J. D. B.

SEE ALSO: GEM, MEASUREMENT

Caraway Caraway is an HERB. It has been known for centuries for its tiny, pungent seed. Caraway seed is used for seasoning foods such as soups, cheese, meats, salads and vegetables. Its most common use is in rye bread.

Caraway is originally from the Old World but has been cultivated in the northern part of the United States. It is a hardy BIENNIAL that is found growing in any kind of soil. Caraway will grow two feet (.61 meter) tall, has beautiful, feathery leaves and creamy or whitish-yellow flowers.   J.K.K.

Caraway

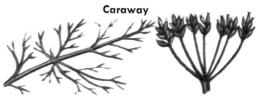

Carbohydrates (car-boh-HY-drates) Carbohydrates are a group of compounds that include all kinds of starches and sugars. They supply most of the energy needed by a living cell. All carbohydrates are changed into simple sugars in the animal digestive tract. In the liver of mammals, most of these are changed into glycogen or animal starch. Glucose can be broken down by cells to give them energy to do their work.

Some of the cells in green plants are the only cells that can make carbohydrates. These cells take carbon dioxide from the air and combine it with hydrogen from water to make a very simple sugar. Chlorophyll, the pigment that makes plants green, traps light energy from the sun and uses this energy to split apart the molecules of water. From this simple sugar, plants can make and store more complex sugars, starches, proteins, fats, and vitamins. Animals depend, directly or indirectly (by eating other animals), upon the stored food of plants.

Although plants lack digestive tracts, they must digest their stored food back into the simpler compounds in order to obtain energy. Digestion is done by individual plant cells.

Chemically, carbohydrates are combinations of carbon, hydrogen, and oxygen atoms. Usually equal numbers of carbon and oxygen atoms unite with twice as much hydrogen.

J. C. K.

Carbolic acid (kahr-BAHL-ick) Carbolic acid is a colorless, crystalline solid which has an easily recognized odor. Its scientific name is *phenol*. Phenol is extremely poisonous. It destroys human skin and is a nerve poison.

Phenol is prepared by the distillation of COAL TAR, or, on a large commercial scale, by a synthetic process. It is used chiefly as a disinfectant, and in the preparation of some plastics. *Picric acid,* a derivative of phenol, is an ingredient in many high explosives. Phenol also has application in the manufacture of dyes, medicines, plant hormones, weed killers, and tanning agents.   D. L. D.

Carbon Carbon is a common chemical element. Large amounts of it are found in the free state in nature. The DIAMOND is the purest form of carbon. It exists as an eight-sided CRYSTAL. When pure, it is colorless, transparent, and brilliant. Inferior quality diamonds are used industrially for glass cutting, grinding, and on the points of drills. This is because the diamond is the hardest substance known. Diamonds can only be cut by other diamonds, and polished with diamond powder.

A piece of strawberry shortcake contains the three main types of carbohydrates—*disaccharides*, or double sugars (in the form of *lactose* from the whipped cream); *fructose*, a simple sugar from the strawberries; and starch, a *polysaccharide*, in the cake.

When this is eaten, the salivary enzymes change the cooked starch to a double sugar, as the first step in the breakdown. In the alimentary canal, the double sugars are hydrolyzed, or turned into simple sugars, by the action of enzymes. These simple sugars are accumulated in the intestine until they are sufficiently concentrated. Then they are absorbed into the blood stream which carries them through the portal vein to the liver.

In the liver, the simple sugar is converted into glycogen by hormones and enzymes. The carbohydrates can be stored as fat or disposed of as energy. The liver regulates a cycle in which it releases glycogen to the blood stream. Some of this is carried to the muscles and stored.

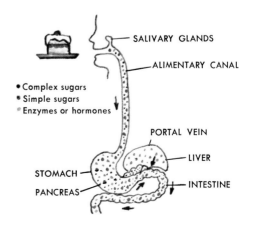

✳ THINGS TO DO

COLLECTING CARBON FROM OXIDATION

1 **With a clamp position a spoon or coin over the flame of a candle. Soon it will have a black deposit on it.**
2 **The candle is made of carbon and hydrogen. When a cold object is placed near it reduces temperature preventing complete oxidation.**
3 **The carbon not burned collects on the spoon or coin.**

If a diamond were heated to a very high temperature (2000+ degrees), in the absence of air, it would be changed to GRAPHITE. Graphite is another crystalline form of carbon, and unlike the diamond, is a very soft substance. When mixed with clay and baked, it becomes the "lead" of lead pencils. Non-crystalline carbon is called *amorphous* (without definite form).

Other impure forms of carbon exist, such as COAL, coke, lampblack, bone black and charcoal. Coal has many varieties, each differing from the others largely as to the degree of CARBONIZATION that has taken place. The varieties such as anthracite, bituminous, lignite and peat are used as fuels and as the starting point for other organic compounds. COKE is the main product formed when bituminous coal is heated in the absence of air. It is used in the manufacture of gases, carbon compounds, and as a fuel. LAMPBLACK is produced when carbon compounds, oils, or natural gas are burned in the absence of

sufficient air for complete combustion, and the smoky gas flame is then chilled. The very finely divided black carbon, also called *carbon black* or *soot,* is used in large quantities in manufacturing printer's INK, phonograph records, and as a black pigment for shoe polish, black paints, and carbon paper. *Bone black,* or *animal charcoal,* is produced when animal bones undergo destructive distillation. It is only about 15% carbon, but because it is so porous, it absorbs large quantities of gases and coloring matter from solutions. CHARCOAL results from the destructive DISTILLATION of wood. *Activated charcoal,* prepared from coconut shells, wood, or coal, is used in gas masks as the particles can adsorb most poisonous gases.

Carbon is found in all living tissues, combined with hydrogen, oxygen and nitrogen. The energy of both plant and animal life is derived from the oxidation of carbon compounds, such as the sugars and starches in the body. Carbon gives man food and clothing, since it is the basis upon which all animal and vegetable tissues are built. Green grass, hay, honey and starch all contain carbon. It is present in tea, coffee, bread, vinegar, butter, and almost every other article of food. Cotton and wool contain much carbon. Carbon provides most of man's FUEL. In coal, kerosene, oil, fat, lard, suet, blubber, or wood, carbon is one of the elements that unites with oxygen, giving off heat and light.

Carbon is so important that the some eight hundred thousand carbon compounds are studied as a separate branch of chemistry, called *organic chemistry.* Within this branch, many compounds have been synthesized in the laboratory to form important drugs, dyes and plastics. Beside these, there is a considerable quantity of mineral CARBONATES distributed throughout the earth. They have many industrial applications.

In 1961, an international agreement of chemists designated *carbon-12,* an isotope, as the standard atomic weight of all 105 elements. Until that time, a natural mixture of oxygen isotopes, with a weight of 16.000, was used. So regular carbon (chemical symbol C), with atomic number 6, is given atomic weight 12.01115. With oxygen as the standard, it was 12.011. C^{12}, the standard, has atomic weight 12.000.   D.L.D.

SEE ALSO: ATOM, CARBON CYCLE, CARBON LIFE, ELEMENTS IN THE HUMAN BODY, HYDROCARBON, ORGANIC COMPOUNDS

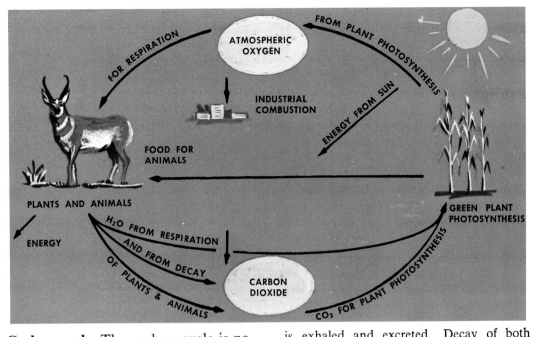

Carbon cycle The carbon cycle is nature's way of adjusting the amounts of carbon and oxygen, so that both ELEMENTS will remain in proper balance. Humans need oxygen to breathe, and they exhale CARBON DIOXIDE, a carbon compound, as a waste product. Green plants, on the other hand, need carbon dioxide in order to make food, but they release OXYGEN as their waste product. If the processes which require oxygen from the atmosphere continued indefinitely without other processes to absorb the carbon dioxide—the waste product of these reactions—the atmosphere would be so heavily concentrated with carbon dioxide that it would no longer be habitable.

The cycle described above is a very incomplete one. Actually, much more is involved beside PHOTOSYNTHESIS and respiration. Carbon dioxide is returned to the atmosphere whenever organic substances are consumed—whether it be by fire, by body energy, or by decay. This encompasses many processes. When coal or wood are consumed by fire, carbon dioxide is produced. When men or animals consume the food-fuel of their bodies, carbon dioxide is exhaled and excreted. Decay of both plant and animal life after death produces carbon dioxide. The process of FERMENTATION supplies carbon dioxide, and the same gas issues from volcanoes and from the soil in regions which are no longer volcanic.

Plants utilize carbon dioxide from the air and water absorbed by their roots. With the sun's energy and the green pigment, CHLOROPHYLL, a chemical reaction results to form a carbohydrate, out of which the plant builds its own body. The waste product, oxygen, is released. Thus, the sun's energy is stored in the plant. Some of the carbon dioxide in the atmosphere goes into the waters of the ocean. This is used by water animals in the building of shells (calcium carbonate).

The materials of the plant bodies are eaten by men and animals and so built into human and animal tissue. Whenever man consumes any part of a plant, the energy stored in that carbohydrate is now able to work for him in active living. With this energy release, carbon dioxide is formed again—and the entire cycle repeats. Some carbon compounds are not readily attacked by animals and microorganisms, and a slight but steady loss of carbon to sediments has produced an accumulation of COAL and PETROLEUM products. However, once these products are burned, carbon dioxide is again formed, keeping the balance intact.   D. L. D.

SEE ALSO: BALANCE OF NATURE, CARBON LIFE

HOW CAN CARBON DIOXIDE BE PRODUCED?

Accepting the fact that fire will not burn in air which is highly concentrated with carbon dioxide, one can test the combination of two materials which release carbon dioxide.

1 Combine baking soda and vinegar in a cup. Light a match and hold it over the solution. The flame will be extinguished.

2 Repeat the experiment above substituting lemon juice and either lime chips, chalk, or egg shells for the two materials to be combined.

3 Mix yeast in warm sugar water. This plant feeds on the sugar releasing carbon dioxide and alcohol. Hold a lighted match over the mixture to test for this release.

4 Lime water becomes cloudy when combined with carbon dioxide. Using a straw, blow air into a glass of limewater. Notice the color before and after. We exhale carbon dioxide.

5 Burning will produce carbon dioxide. Burn a candle which has been placed in a jar with a small amount of limewater. After several minutes extinguish the flame, cover the jar, and shake lightly. The limewater becomes cloudy.

Carbon dioxide Carbon dioxide is a colorless, tasteless gas, widely distributed in nature. It is a vital part of the CARBON CYCLE. Carbon dioxide is obtained from natural wells, from direct manufacture, and from chemical processes as a by-product as in the fermentation of grain.

Carbon dioxide has a large assortment of uses. As a solid, called "DRY ICE," it is a better refrigerant than ice because it evaporates directly to a gas and has an extremely low temperature, making it particularly useful in frozen food industries and in preservation of perishables. Gaseous carbon dioxide, which has a blanketing effect on fire and reduces the temperature below the ignition point, is used extensively in FIRE EXTINGUISHERS. Carbonated beverages (soda water) provide a big market for carbon dioxide. It gives "bite" to the drink by forming the weak carbonic acid. As a pressure medium for instantaneous inflation, small carbon dioxide cartridges are packaged with life rafts and preservers. Carbon dioxide is used chemically in leavening agents, such as baking powder, and in neutralizing water in water-softening plants. Manufacturing paint, electric arc welding, and commercially preparing and packaging foods all require the use of carbon dioxide.   D.L.D.

Carbon life Modern science recognizes that all forms of life must be based on certain chemical processes. The term "chemical process" means a reaction or sequence of reactions of atoms or molecules. In the course of the chemical process, heat is either generated or absorbed.

Simple chemical reactions are the burning of HYDROGEN (H_2) and OXYGEN (O_2) to water (H_2O), or the burning of CARBON (C) in oxygen to form CARBON DIOXIDE (CO_2) or else CARBON MONOXIDE (CO) if the combustion is not complete. In both cases, heat is generated by taking elements (such as the atom C or the molecules H_2, O_2) and combining them to form COMPOUNDS. Compounds are combinations of two or more elements. Therefore, they almost always consist of bigger and more complex molecules than the ELEMENTS.

Lifeless (inorganic) compounds consist of relatively small molecules, mostly containing far less than 100 atoms. The reason for this is that most elements are "choosey," that is, they combine only with a small number of other elements. The two major exceptions are the elements SILICON and carbon. The *affinity* (willingness to form compounds with other elements) of carbon by far exceeds that of silicon.

Life substances (ORGANIC COMPOUNDS) consist of very large, complex molecules, containing many hundreds and even thousands of atoms and a great number of elements, although they are mostly carbon and hydrogen. Of these two, carbon forms the basic structure of the large organic molecules. This applies to all forms of life on Earth and, therefore, they are often referred to as *carbon life*.

The strength of carbon has two advantages. Firstly, it lends great stability to the large organic molecules. Secondly, carbon's affinity to other elements helps in preventing slow poisoning of living organisms. A POISON is a chemical substance which for some reason is incompatible with the organic substance or with the functioning of a living organism. If a poison, however, is consumed in very small quantities, it may not be effective (harmful).

Under everyday conditions, tiny quantities of poison enter living organisms all the time. If permitted to accumulate, they could be deadly. Actually, they are either discharged or chemically destroyed, because the affinity of carbon breaks the bonds which hold the hostile molecules together, thereby rendering the substance harmless.

Technically speaking, all living organisms are little heat engines. If enough people or animals fill a cold room, it soon becomes noticeably warmer. Moving organisms (animals and man) especially need energy which is generated by the combustion of food in the body. The required oxygen enters the blood through the lungs, combustion products are discharged through the bowels (solid), through the kidneys and skin pores (liquid) and through the lungs (gaseous, such as CO_2 and water vapor). Thus, animals consume oxygen. Land animals take oxygen out of the air, sea animals take it out of the water. Land animals would suffocate within minutes in an atmosphere which contains no oxygen, sea animals would similarly suffocate in a fluid which contains no oxygen, for instance, in a sea of oil.

Plants, the other principal form of earth life, are generally thought of as generating, but not consuming, oxygen. It is, however, more correct to say that plants do not require free oxygen like land animals do. Plants can absorb CO_2, break it apart and thereby set the oxygen free. They do need a small quantity of O_2 for their own respiration. Most of it they discharge into the atmosphere and thereby make it "breathable" for the animals. Thus, plants and animals complement each other; plants discharge free oxygen and animals discharge CO_2. The life of animals depends on plants; but, since there are many sources of CO_2 (for example, volcanoes), plants do not need animals for their existence.

History of life on this planet indicates

indeed that plants were the first forms of life to inhabit the oceans and the first to conquer the land. Since the earth's AT-MOSPHERE contains a much higher percentage of free oxygen than the atmospheres of other planets, one may suspect that this is the result of plants decomposing CO_2 and discharging the O_2 into the atmosphere for many millions of years (while the carbon finally became coal). Not until the plants made the air breathable, could carbon life develop outside the oceans.   K. A. E.

SEE ALSO: SILICON LIFE

Carbon monoxide

Carbon monoxide is a colorless, odorless, poisonous gas. It forms readily when carbon substances burn in a low air supply.

The gas, formula *CO,* is widely used in smelting to separate a metal from its ore—as in extracting IRON in a blast furnace and in refining nickel. It is important in industrial preparations of many organic chemicals. The proportions of *CO* present both in natural and artificial gas add to the heat yield of these fuels.

Because the gas is odorless, care is needed wherever it may be present. Greatest dangers arise from leaky furnaces and car engines running in closed garages. Researches on tobacco smoking indicate that traces of this gas inhaled by smokers contribute to the health hazards of the habit.

Inhaled carbon monoxide enters the BLOOD and prevents the red cells from absorbing oxygen needed by body tissues.   D. A. B.

Carbon tetrachloride

(tet-trah-KLO-ride) Carbon tetrachloride is a colorless, pleasant-smelling, non-flammable liquid which is composed of carbon and chlorine. It is manufactured by chemical reaction.

Once carbon tetrachloride was used extensively as a dry cleaning agent and in fire extinguishers. Medically it was used as an anesthetic and to control hookworms. Due to its toxic nature, it has been banned from clinical use by the U.S. Food and Drug Administration. Its use as a cleaning agent and in fire extinguishers is no longer recommended because its fumes have been tied to cancer. The fumes also cause liver and kidney damage. Its main use is in the production of *freons.*   A.J.H./D.L.D.

 THINGS TO DO

DOES CARBON DIOXIDE PUT OUT FIRE?

Materials: atomizer or spray bottle, cake pan, saturated sodium bicarbonate solution (baking soda).

1   This should be done ONLY when an older person is helping.

2   Fill an atomizer or spray bottle half full of a saturated solution of sodium bicarbonate (baking soda).

3   Crumple up a small piece of newspaper, place it in a cake pan, and set it on fire.

4   Spray the flames with the solution. The fire goes out.

5   Carbon dioxide is released from the sodium bicarbonate solution. It smothers the fire and prevents oxygen from getting to it.

Carbonates Carbonates are COM-POUNDS in which a metal combines with a special grouping of one part carbon to three parts oxygen, known as the carbonate ion (CO_3^{--}), to form a salt. Carbonic acid (H_2CO_3), the familiar "soda water," contains this carbonate ion. It is sometimes used commercially in a chemical reaction to produce a desired carbonate. Carbonates are found widely distributed in nature. For example, CALCIUM CARBONATE ($CaCO_3$) exists as CALCITE, marble, limestone, and in fish shells. The common rock, DOLOMITE, is a double carbonate of magnesium and calcium [$CaMg(CO_3)_2$].

Sodium carbonate (Na_2CO_3), commonly known as washing soda, is used in the manufacture of glass, paper, and textiles, and as a household cleaning agent. Basic lead carbonate, $2PbCO_3Pb(OH)_2$, or white lead, was used as a white pigment in oil based paints. Carbonates of iron, called *siderite* ($FeCO_3$); of manganese, called *rhodochrosite* ($Mn CO_3$); of magnesium, called *magnesite* ($MgCO_3$); and of zinc, called *smithsonite* ($ZnCO_3$) are all common. There are many other carbonate compounds.

Carbonates are insoluble in water, except those of sodium, potassium, and ammonium. When heated, carbonates break down to their oxides and carbon dioxide. A carbonate can be converted to a bicarbonate by reacting it with carbonic acid. Sodium carbonate, Na_2CO_3, plus carbonic acid, H_2CO_3, yields sodium bicarbonate, $NaHCO_3$.   A.J.H.
SEE ALSO: SODIUM BICARBONATE

Carboniferous age see Geologic time table

Carbonization The term *carbonization* generally refers to three processes. Since these processes are somewhat different, it is best to discuss each process individually.

(1) The most common usage of the term involves transforming organic matter into CHARCOAL, a residue of carbon, by fire or a corrosive chemical. The distillation of COAL is the heating of bituminous coal in the absence of air to obtain coke and other valuable by-products.

Temperature determines which carbonization by-products will result. High-temperature carbonization of coal (1000-1300° C. or 1832°-2882° F.) yields AMMONIA, fuel gas, light oil, and COAL TAR as by-products of coke. Low-temperatures (400-750° C. 752°-1562° F.) produces by-products of PETROLEUM, gas, and large amounts of coal tar and liquids.

(2) Carbonization also refers to a textile process of removing vegetable matter from wool. The matter may be burrs, bark, grass and cotton fibers. These organic impurities are destroyed by acids or salts, reduced to carbon, and removed by mechanical means.

(3) An entirely different process—that of combining, covering, or impregnating a substance with carbon is still another definition of carbonization. An example of this process is the "cementation" process for making STEEL.   D. L. D.

Carburetor (KAHR-buh-ray-ter) A carburetor is an apparatus in which air or gas is mixed with carbon compounds which can easily turn into vapor. This mixture of gas and carbon compounds can produce more energy than can the gas or carbon alone. In an AUTOMOBILE carburetor, air is mixed with gasoline spray (a carbon compound) to produce an easily exploded mixture.
SEE: ENGINES

Carcinoma see Cancer (disease)

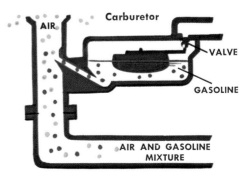

Cardinal climber

Carcinogen (kahr-SIN-uh-jin) A carcinogen is anything that causes CANCER. Some airborne carcinogens are tobacco smoke, asbestos dust, and vinyl chloride gas. Certain chemicals, including tars and some dyes, and RADIATION (including radiation from the sun) seem to be carcinogens.

Many substances appear to be carcinogenic when laboratory animals are exposed to them in large doses. Deciding which carcinogens pose a threat to the public is difficult. Most people, for example, are exposed to only tiny amounts of vinyl chloride gas. But workers in factories manufacturing polyvinyl chloride (a type of plastic) were once exposed to much larger quantities. For those workers, the carcinogen posed a greater risk. Recent studies suggest a link between HEREDITY and some types of cancer. J.H.

SEE ALSO: AEROSOL, AIR POLLUTION, ASBESTOS

Cardinal The cardinal is a beautiful rosy-red bird with a crest on its head. Its bill is also red and cone-shaped. The bird ranges from 7 to 9 inches (17.8 to 22.9 centimeters). Its loud warbling whistle or its short "cheer-cheer" can be heard all year around for it does not migrate. Some cardinals live all their lives in one place.

The female bird is a light brownish-gray color. She sings as well as the male, which is unusual for female birds.

Cardinals like to nest in thick tangled bushes near the edges of woods. After a nest is built of twigs and small roots and lined with grass, the female lays three or four eggs which are pale blue or gray and spotted. Cardinals eat both insects and seeds and berries. Sunflower seeds will attract them to a feeder.

Cardinal climber The long stem of this vine needs a fence or trellis to hang on to. The leaves are finely and deeply lobed. The scarlet red flower is shaped like a trumpet.

This annual hybrid was produced by crossing two species of the morning glory plant. The stem is about 15 feet (4.57 meters) long. The flower, which has five united petals, blooms in summer. The fruit is a round pod. It is in the family Convolvulaceae. H.J.C.

Cardiograph see Electrocardiograph

Cardiovascular system see Circulatory system

Caribou see Deer family

Caries see Tooth decay

Carnation Carnation is a plant that blooms in the fall. It grows 2 or 3 feet (.61 to .91 meters) tall. There are over 2000 varieties of carnations and they have been grown for over 20 centuries. It is the state flower of Ohio.

The narrow, gray-blue leaves are arranged opposite to each other on a rather brittle, long stem. The doubled flowers are usually red, white, or pink. The green ones have been dyed for St. Patrick's Day. Plants may be annuals, biennials or perennials.

The enemies of this plant include stem rot, rust, red spider and wilt. Soil sterilization and spray will usually help get rid of the fungus and insect pests. H. J. C.

A male cardinal
Mrs. Allen D. Cruickshank

Carnation

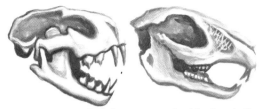

A carnivore skull (left) compared with the skull of a plant-eating animal

Carnivore (KAHR-nuh-vore) The cat, dog, bear, skunk and seal are among the three hundred different mammals called carnivores. These animals eat a great deal of meat, and that is why they are called *carni-* (flesh) *vore* (eating).

The words carnivore and carnivorous are used to describe the food habits of any meat-eating animal. Mammals in the order Carnivora are all meat eaters. All carnivores do not belong to this order. Mosquitoes and fleas are carnivores, but belong to the insect group.

All animals of Order *Carnivora* eat meat, but there is considerable variety in the diet of different animals. Those carnivores with webbed feet, the seal, sea lion and walrus, are specially fitted for swimming and eat fish. The group with separate toes includes all other carnivores. The cat-like and dog-like animals are excellent hunters and often eat only meat. The bears, however, eat vegetables as well as meat in their diet. The skunk is particularly fond of eggs and meats while his relatives, the weasel and mink, often hunt just for the joy of killing. The raccoon eats everything from clams and fish to fruit and vegetables.

Carnivores have no single characteristic which separates them from all other mammals. They are classified on the basis of many physical features. Most have five toes on each foot, and none has fewer than four. Usually they have claws on their toes and two tufts of very sensitive whiskers (*vibrissae*) on their cheeks. They have six incisor teeth and two long canine teeth in both upper and lower jaws. Their cheek teeth are blade-like and snip past each other like scissors. Like man, carnivores have two sets of teeth in their lifetimes. J. L. K.

Carnotite Carnotite is an ore of URANIUM. It contains some radium. It is a yellow crystalline powder found mainly in sandstone deposits, and as a crust on sedimentary rocks.

Carotene see Vitamin

Carotid artery see Circulatory system

Chicago Natural History Museum
Carp

Carp Carp were originally European freshwater fish. When brought to America, they spread all over the continent and developed many *variations* (changes) in color and shape. Colors now range from yellowish to silver, dark green, black, or brown.

Teeth are in the throat rather than in the mouth. Around the mouth are whisker-like appendages called *barbels*. Both dorsal and anal fins are spined. Carp grow to about 3 feet (.91 meters) long and may weight 25 pounds (11.34 kilograms) or more. Carp prefer muddy-bottomed streams and feed on plants and animals in the mud. A relative is the aquarium goldfish. J.C.K.

Carpel see Pistil

Carrier wave A carrier wave is a high frequency radio wave. Some characteristic of it is changed or modulated in accordance with another wave so that music or speech is transmitted.
SEE: RADIO, SOUND, TELEVISION

Carriers Carriers are individuals who carry DISEASE germs in their bodies. They have already had the disease, and are no longer ill (or are immune.) Carriers can pass the disease on to other people.

Carrot

Carrot It is an herb that grows a large fleshy root, yellow or orange in color. It may be 6 inches (15.24 centimeters) long. Sugar and vitamins are stored in the root. The leaves are green and lacy. The small flower is white.

The carrot has pinnately compound leaves. It is a biennial plant. The first year food is stored in the taproot. The second year a flower stalk appears. Flowers are perfect, having five petals, sepals, and stamens. The flowers form umbrella-like clusters. The ovary matures into a dry indehiscent FRUIT with one oblong, flat seed, an achene. The yellow pigment in the root is *carotin* and is used to color oleomargarine.

Carrots belong to the Umbelliferae family. Queen Anne's lace is the wild carrot from which the garden variety developed.   H. J. C.

Cartilage tissue (KAR-tuh-lij) Cartilage is a tough, semitransparent solid tissue. Its common name is *gristle*. It is found on the ends of long bones, in the nose, the outer ear, and other places in the body. Most of the skeleton is formed first in cartilage and later replaced by bone. Cartilage cells secrete the solid portion, trapping themselves in holes or *lacunae*. The solid part of the cartilage is called the *matrix*. The walls of the lacunae are called capsules.

Cartilage cells are found among connective tissues. Thus the matrix of cartilage always contains some kind of connective tissue fiber. Hyaline, or glasslike cartilage, has as a base *collagenous* (fine and white) fibers. These fibers cannot be seen in the glasslike matrix. This type of cartilage is found most often in the body. Examples are the tracheal rings and the ends of ribs.

Elastic cartilage is found in the *larynx* (voice box) and outer ear. Elastic cartilage is yellowish, less transparent, and more flexible. In its matrix are coarse, branched, yellow elastic fibers.

Fibrocartilage is found mainly in the disks between the vertebrae. Dense bundles of wavy white connective tissue fibers appear in the matrix.   J. C. K.

SEE ALSO: HISTOLOGY, SKELETON

Civil Air Patrol
A flat map of the earth's surface

Cartography Cartography is the science of preparing maps and charts that show the earth's round surface on a flat area.

A map is based upon a *map projection,* of which there are many different types. A map projection is a system of parallels and meridians drawn on a flat surface to represent the earth's spherical geographic grid.

Maps and charts are drawn to scale. As an example, one inch of a map might be equal to one mile on the surface of the area being mapped. Various types of symbols to show surface features are also used.   H. S. G.

SEE ALSO: MAP MAKING, PROJECTION

Carver, George Washington (1864?–1943) Carver was an American agricultural chemist. Born in slavery, he lived to enjoy international fame. Forty-five years of his life he spent at Tuskegee Institute in Alabama working on new ways to help the South restore its land. The soil had been worn out by the continual growing of COTTON. Carver encouraged the planting of peanuts and sweet potatoes to nourish and restore the soil. Carver experimented in his laboratory and discovered over 300 uses of the peanut and more than 125 uses of the sweet potato.

Among the products that he made from peanuts were wood dyes, soap, shampoo, linoleum and metal polish, ink, cooking oils, peanut butter, and cheese. From the sweet potato he created such products as a valuable rubber compound, starch, imitation ginger, library paste, vinegar, wood filler, rope, and instant coffee.

About the time of the official emancipation of the slaves, George Washington Carver was born to slave parents on the farm of Moses Carver in Diamond Grove, Missouri. His father was killed shortly before his birth, and when he was about six months old, Night Raiders kidnapped him and his mother. No one knows what happened to the young mother, but the baby was returned to Moses Carver by a man who found the child abandoned on the road, desperately ill with whooping cough. This disease affected his voice so that it remained high and thin all his life.

After Carver was graduated from Iowa State College at Ames with a Master's degree in agriculture, he continued to teach at the college. He received many invitations to teach in southern schools, but he considered none until Booker T. Washington asked him to come to Tuskegee Institute to teach, do research, and help the neighboring farmers reclaim their land. He found great satisfaction in his laboratory, for he was a quiet man who did not like crowds or public acclaim. When THOMAS A. EDISON offered him over $50,000 a year to work in his laboratory in California, Carver refused. Money meant nothing to him. He never accepted an increase in salary at Tuskegee, and he often did not cash the salary checks he did receive. He never applied for a patent on his discoveries because he said, "God gave them to me. Why should I claim them for my own?" D. H. J.

Cashmere The cashmere is a goat. Originally it lived in the Valley of Kashmir and in the Himalaya Mountains. They can now be found in both China and Tibet. The goat is short-legged, horned, and graceful.

Cashmeres are valued for their fine, thick undercoats. The undercoat is combed out and used to make wool. Expensive sweaters, coats, and shawls are made from the wool.

These goats belong to the cattle family Bovidae. They are cud chewers and grazers. Relatives are sheep and antelopes. J. C. K.
SEE ALSO: ANTELOPE, GOAT, SHEEP

Casein see Dairy products, Paints

Cashew see Nuts

Cassia see Cinnamon

Cassiopeia

Cassiopeia (kass-ee-uh-PEE-uh) Cassiopeia is a group of stars that looks like a W or an M in the sky. Ancient people thought it looked like a chair or a woman in a chair. Cassiopeia is near POLARIS, the North Star. In the northern part of the world it can be seen on most nights of the year.

Cassiopeia was the name of the wife of CEPHEUS, who was king of Ethiopia. They had a daughter named Andromeda. The three members of this royal family are all immortalized in constellations. Cassiopeia was a very beautiful woman. She was also vain. She boasted that she was more beautiful than the sea nymphs. The sea nymphs were insulted and they complained to the god of the sea, Neptune. Neptune decided to punish Cassiopeia by having a terrible monster attack the coast of Ethiopia. Cepheus went to the oracle of Jupiter to find out how to get rid of the monster. The oracle told him that he would have to sacrifice his daughter Andromeda to the monster. Cepheus chained Andromeda to a rock along the shore for the monster. Andromeda was saved by Perseus, who is also immortalized in a constellation.

Some legends say that the sea nymphs were angry when Cassiopeia was given a place in the sky. They asked Jupiter to arrange it so that she would hang upside down part of the night. C. L. K.
SEE ALSO: CONSTELLATIONS

Cassiterite see Tin

Cast iron see Iron

Castor oil Castor oil is made from the seeds, or "castor beans," of the castor-oil plant. It is used in making soaps and paint, for engine oil, and as a medicine acting as a laxative in the intestinal tract.

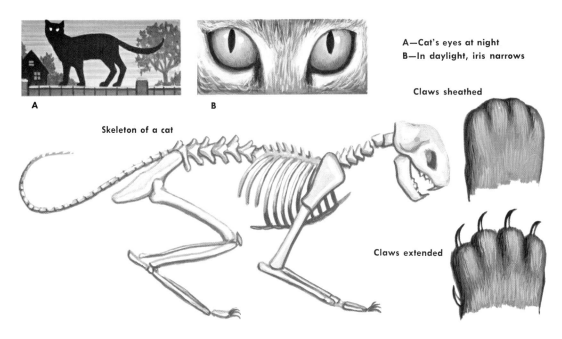

A—Cat's eyes at night
B—In daylight, iris narrows

Claws sheathed

A

B

Skeleton of a cat

Claws extended

Cat family

Cat family All cats, from small, gentle house cats to wild lions and tigers, belong to the same animal family. There are about forty different kinds (species) of cats.

Cats are among the best hunters of the flesh-eating animals (CARNIVORES). The *saber-toothed tiger,* which lived long ago, had a pair of upper teeth 8 inches (20.32 centimeters) long which looked like daggers. It used these dagger-like teeth to kill wild horses, camels, and other animals much larger than itself. Although cats today do not have dagger-like teeth, they are well-equipped for hunting.

CHARACTERISTICS OF CATS

All cats have long, curved CLAWS, with which they can grip and tear the flesh of their prey. They keep these claws sharp by scraping them on tree trunks or other rough surfaces. People who own house cats often give them wooden scratching posts. Most cats' claws can be pulled back (retracted) into folds of skin (*sheaths*) at the ends of their toes. When its claws are retracted, a cat can walk silently.

Cats walk on their toes; their heel bones do not touch the ground. They have five toes on each front foot and four on each back foot. Small pads on their feet cushion their walk and help them to move quietly.

Most cats hunt at night. They are helped by a fairly good sense of smell, keen hearing, and the ability to see very well in dim light. The cells within a cat's eye are very sensitive to light. At night, the colored part (iris) of a cat's eye opens exceptionally wide, letting in extra light and enabling the cat to see better than most other animals. In the day, the iris closes to a thin vertical slit, shutting out the bright light. This is true of cats that hunt at night. Those that hunt during the day, such as the lion and the cheetah, have irises which contract into small circles like those of humans and other animals.

A cat is a graceful animal with excellent control over the muscles of its body. It has over five hundred muscles which it can control and use at will. Its backbone is flexible so it can twist and turn easily. It can climb well and balance itself easily. It can run swiftly for short distances and take great and powerful leaps. After stalking its prey, it leaps, knocks it down, and then bites, tears, or shakes it to death.

Most wild members of the cat family are the color of the dry grass, dead leaves, and bare rock which make up the environment in which they live. They usually have from two to five cubs every other year.

The small cats kept as pets in people's homes are called *house cats*. Cats are not usually as friendly as dogs, and very few can be trained to do tricks and obey orders. However, they are neat, quiet and graceful pets and need less care than dogs. There are two kinds of house cats, shorthair and longhair. Siamese, manx, and stray or alley cats have short hair. Persian cats have long hair. They have heavier bodies than shorthair cats and long, silky coats which grow in great ruffs around their necks. Their toes and ears often have tufts of fur.

Cats shed their coats every spring, summer, and fall and shed their claws at various times during the year. The purring sounds that most cats make when relaxed are from a pair of false "vocal cords" above the true cords. The true cords relax and air is free to vibrate around the membranes of the false cords.

House cats have from four to eight kittens at one time and may have litters as often as two or three times a year. Pet cats should be given a warm, dry box for sleeping and two or three meals each day. Cats keep themselves clean with their rough tongues.

Cats have from thirty to thirty-two teeth, all of which are designed chiefly for cutting and tearing flesh. Flesh is more easily digested than grains and grasses, so the digestive system of the cat is rather simple in comparison with that of a cow or horse.

Cats' eyes glow in the dark because the cells of the retina are coated with a chemical (guanin) which reflects light.

The tabby is distinguished by its beautifully striped hair

Courtesy Society For Visual Education, Inc.
The color in a Siamese cat's hair starts to appear several days after birth

The manx (originally from the Isle of Man) has no visible tail.

F. A. Blashfield
Pure Angoras are very rare. Most of them have been interbred with the long-haired Persian.

Tigers hunt deer, water buffaloes, and young elephants in the jungles and grasslands of Asia

KINDS OF CATS

The earliest ancestor of the cat was the *miacis,* which lived over fifty-five million years ago. The miacis had a long body and tail, short legs, and looked somewhat like a weasel. It gradually developed into an animal that looked like the CIVET, a flesh-eating mammal found in warm areas of Africa and southern Asia. Cats as known today probably appeared on earth about forty million years ago.

The *cheetah,* also called the *hunting leo-pard,* is found in the open country of Africa and Asia. It is about 6 feet (1.83 meters) long and has a rough coat of fairly long, black-spotted yellow fur. Its claws are more blunt than those of other cats and cannot be retracted. The cheetah hunts in the day and is often trained by man for hunting. Known as the world's fastest mammal, it can run up to 70 miles (112.65 kilometers) an hour over short distances. It runs down its prey instead of leaping upon it. Cheetahs hunt deer, antelope, goats, and fowl.

The *puma,* also called the *cougar, moun-tain lion, panther, painter, catamount,* and *kingcat,* is a sandy-colored cat about 6 feet (1.83 meters) long, weighing up to 100 pounds (45.36 kilograms). Once pumas were found all over North America. Now they are found mainly in Florida, the Blue Ridge Mountains, and the wilder parts of western United States. The puma is an excellent climber and can get up into the lower branches of trees with one graceful leap. It hunts and eats elk, deer, mountain beaver, porcupine, rodents, and sometimes cattle and horses. When it is finished eating, it will often cover remaining parts of its prey with sticks and leaves and save it for another day.

The *jaguar* is a wild member of the cat family found mainly in the jungles of Central and South America. It looks very much like a leopard but is heavier and has spots with black rings around them. Jaguars climb well and spend much of their time in trees, hunting birds and monkeys. They also hunt deer, fish, turtles, alligators, and sometimes cattle and horses. Jaguars don't hunt out in the open. They jump on their prey from a hiding place.

The *leopard,* also called a *panther,* is found in Africa, Asia, and parts of Europe. It has a tan coat covered with black spots usually arranged in small groups of five or six. Some leopards have so many spots that they look as if they have black coats. Leopards are about 7 feet (2.13 meters) long and weigh 125 pounds (56.7 kilograms). They hunt monkeys, birds, antelopes, jackals, and snakes. They are very strong and can

Some wild members of the cat family: (from left—top) puma, black leopard; (center) ocelot, male lion, jaguarundi; (bottom) snow leopard, bobcat

leap into trees with prey weighing as much as 80 pounds (36.29 kilograms.)

The *lion,* the "king of beasts," lives in the grasslands and sandy plains of India and Africa. It has yellowish-brown fur, is 8-10 feet (2.44-3.05 meters) long, and weighs about 400 pounds (181.44 kilograms). The male lion has a huge mane and a bushy-tipped tail. Lions hunt alone or in small groups *(prides).* Their prey includes zebras, young elephants, antelopes, and sometimes domestic animals. A lion can break the neck of its prey with one blow of its forelegs. Young lions in the circus are taught simple tricks, but never become really tame.

The Canadian *lynx,* sometimes called a *wildcat* or *true lynx,* has long, silky, brownish-gray fur, a stumpy tail, and tufted ears. It lives in forests and rocky areas of Canada. The soles of its large feet are furred in winter and serve as snowshoes, making it possible for the lynx to walk on the top of the snow. It hunts at night for mice, squirrels, foxes, birds, and hares, especially the snowshoe hare.

The *bay lynx,* or *bobcat,* is smaller than the wildcat. A more southerly animal, it is found in the rocky areas of the United States. It has brownish-gray fur with black spots and a short bobbed tail from which

it gets its name. Bobcats prey on wood rats, mice, rabbits, muskrats, squirrels, and sometimes deer and sheep.

The *ocelot* looks like a very big house cat. It is about 50 inches (127 centimeters) long, weighs 30 pounds (13.61 kilograms), and has gray and tan fur marked in definite patterns of spots and stripes. This beautiful cat lives in the forests of Central and South America. Ocelots hunt and eat lizards, monkeys, snakes, birds, rabbits, rats, mice, sheep, and pigs. They are the most gentle of the wild cats and are often tamed and kept as house pets.

Tigers are very large cats with yellow fur and black stripes. They are about 8-10 feet (2.44-3.05 meters) long and weight as much as 400 pounds (181.44 kilograms). They are found in the jungle and grasslands of Asia. Tigers hunt by night for deer, antelope, water buffalo, and young elephants. They kill not only for food but also for the love of blood. Tigers have been known to kill people when other food has been scarce. They are excellent swimmers and good climbers.

Other wild members of the cat family include the caracal, European wildcat, golden cat, jaguarundi, margay, ounce, palla's cat, and the serval. D.J.A.

Catabolism see Metabolism

Catalpa

Catalpa (kuh-TAL-puh) The catalpa is a tall, stately shade tree much used in parks and gardens for its beauty. It is often called the *Indian bean tree* because its seeds grow in long narrow pods like giant string beans.

Catalpa trees grow in the United States, the West Indies, and China. They belong to the *bignonia* or *trumpet-creeper* family.

The tree has a short trunk and a broad dome-topped pyramidal shape. It grows to 60 feet (18.29 meters) in height.

The leaves are heart-shaped with a fuzzy underside. The flowers which grow in pointed clusters, are bell-shaped and are white streaked with brown. The bark is thin, scaly, and furrowed. The wood is dark brown and soft but very durable, often being used for fence posts because it does not rot readily.

Pests that attack the catalpa are the catalpa midge, the catalpa sphinx caterpillar, and the mealy bug.   J. M. C.

Catalyst (KAT-uh-list) A catalyst, or *catalytic agent,* is a chemical which changes the speed of reaction of two or more other chemicals. In this process, the catalyst is not itself permanently changed. The most often used catalysts hasten reactions, but others may slow them. Catalysts produced in living plants or animals are ORGANIC CHEMICALS called ENZYMES. *Pepsin* is such an organic catalyst.

Catalysts are called *positive* or *negative,* depending on whether they *speed* up or *slow* down a chemical reaction.

Catalysis plays an important part in industrial chemistry. A great number of chemicals are produced by catalytic processes. Platinum, for example, is a valuable commercial catalyst, used in many reactions. Platinum powder or platinized asbestos is used in the preparation of sulfuric acid. Platinum gauze is used in preparing nitric acid. Zinc oxide and copper (or other catalysts) are used in manufacturing methanol. Thousands of catalysts exist. Even water is one. Catalysts in living systems are called ENZYMES. Bacteria and molds are used in industry as biological catalysts.

Catalysts are used in two different situations: (1) to increase a rate already detectable without a catalyst, and (2) to encourage the substances reacting to form several different products (only one or none of which would occur at detectable rates without a catalyst). In this second situation, the choice that is made as to which product (or products) should be formed is called *selectivity.* For example, when carbon monoxide and hydrogen react under carefully controlled temperature and pressure conditions, the variation of catalysts produces varied results. With nickel as a catalyst, the result is methane and water. With cobalt and thorium dioxide as catalysts, the main products are methane, ethane, propane, butane, pentane, water and others. Other catalysts produce still more products.

The catalyst may be in the same physical state as the substances reacting (*homogeneous* catalysis), or in a different state (*heterogeneous* catalysis).   D. L. D.

✳ THINGS TO DO

CAN A CHEMICAL CHANGE BE SPEEDED UP?

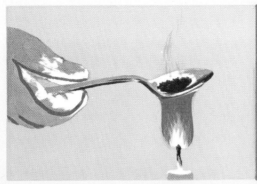
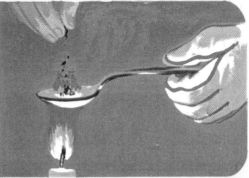

1   **Wearing an insulated glove, hold a tablespoon of sugar over a flame. Permit it to burn. It will melt and turn brown but will not blaze up.**

2   **Repeat the experiment, only this time**

mix ashes in the sugar. Now the sugar will burn freely.

3   **The ash is a catalyst to hasten oxidation but does not change in form as the sugar does.**

Cataract (KATT-uh-rackt) Cataract is a disease of the EYE affecting the lens. The lens is a semisolid substance that is enclosed in a capsule. It is a growing tissue composed of layers much like those of an onion. Normally, these layers are transparent. In cataract, one or more layers of the lens become opaque and will not transmit light.

Cataracts are classified according to their origin. *Developmental* cataracts result from heredity, malnutrition, or inflammation before or near the time of birth. A VIRUS infection during pregnancy may cause cataracts in a child. The *degenerative* cataract is caused by exposure to heat rays, chemicals, disease, or radiation. *Senile* cataracts are found in persons of old age. *Traumatic* cataracts are caused either by a sharp object piercing or penetrating the eye, or by a severe blow to the head which jars the eye. DIABETES hastens the development of cataracts in one or both eyes.

No medication yet known restores transparency to the lens. When the lens becomes opaque, the only remedy is surgical removal of the cataract. Artificial lenses can now be implanted in the eye to restore vision almost perfectly.   B.M.H.

Catbird   Members of the Thrasher family are catbirds, mockingbirds, and thrashers. These birds have slender bodies and longish bills with hairlike bristles around the base. Catbirds are slate gray with black crowns.

The catbird's only spot of color is a patch of rusty red underneath the tail. Their wings are rounded and short. Their tails are medium length. The middle and outer front toes of the catbird are partly fused. Catbirds are primarily found in the western United States and Canada.

Like the mockingbird, the catbird can mimic many of the birds in its vicinity. Its own call is a catlike meow.

The nests of sticks, grass, leaves, and rootlets are built in thickets which are close to the ground. Eggs are blue-green and hatch in 12 to 13 days after they are laid. The male catbird will often help the female in brooding the developing eggs. This is rare among birds.

      J. C. K.

Catbird

Mrs. Allan D. Cruickshank

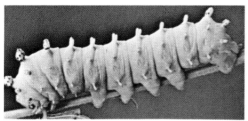

A common caterpillar

Caterpillar The *larvae* (young) of moths and butterflies are called caterpillars. Since they crawl, they look like worms. They are not worms because they have six legs and chewing mouthparts. All caterpillars have a distinct head, a thorax of three segments, and an abdomen of ten segments.

Legs are on the thorax. Some caterpillars have fleshly abdominal prolegs, but these are not true legs. The "skin" may be fuzzy, smooth, or bristly. The head bears a pair of *antennae* (feelers) and a few simple eyes.

Caterpillars usually eat vegetation. A few, like the clothes moth, eat animal products. As they grow, they molt, finally pupating in the fall. In the spring, they emerge as adult butterflies and moths.   J. C. K.

SEE ALSO: LARVA, METAMORPHOSIS

Catfish Catfish is a large group of fish with long feelers (*barbels*) which look a little like cat's whiskers. They have sharp spines on the front of their back (dorsal) and breast (pectoral) fins. Sometimes these spines are poisonous. Catfish have no scales.

Catfish are fresh-water fish. They live near the muddy bottom of lakes, rivers, ponds and streams. Their long feelers move all the time, searching for food. Catfish eat both dead and living things. They also eat the waste from fish and water animals.

There are over a thousand different kinds of catfish. Some, such as blue catfish, weigh over 100 pounds (45.36 kilograms). Others are so tiny they can be raised in an aquarium with goldfish or other small fish. Many catfish are edible.   D.J.A.

Channel catfish

Cathode A cathode is a negatively charged terminal point of an electrical circuit. In ELECTROLYSIS, the conductors that dip into the solution are called ELECTRODES, instead of terminals. The cathode is the negative electrode whereby the current enters the solution. The cathode's counterpart is the positively charged ANODE where the current leaves the solution and electrons enter the wires, to flow back to the cathode.

Similarly, electron tubes contain a small metal cathode that accepts electrons from the circuit. It, in turn, emits an electron stream to the anode in order to conduct the electrical current necessary for the tube's operation. In a simple voltaic cell, the cathode may be just a zinc bar.   E. I. D.

SEE ALSO: CATHODE-RAY TUBE, ELECTRON, ELECTRONICS, TELEVISION

Cathode ray A cathode ray is a stream of ELECTRONS (negatively charged particles) emitted from the cathode of a gas discharge tube. The cathode ray is used in fluorescent lamps, neon tubes, kinescope or TELEVISION picture tubes, and oscilloscopes. The ray excites luminescent materials and causes them to glow. In this process, electrical energy is changed to visible radiation.

In the early 19th century, a German glassblower, Heinrich Geissler, made a glass tube which he filled with a gas at very low pressure. By sparking the tube with high voltage, he made the tube glow. When a British scientist, Sir William Crookes, experimented further by removing most of the gas, he found that the glow almost disappeared. He noticed, however, that a shadow of the center electrical terminal appeared at the end of the tube when this terminal was connected to the positive side of the high voltage and the other terminal was connected to the negative side. When the connections were reversed, *no shadow appeared*. He concluded that either invisible rays or particles were produced at the negative post and interrupted by the positive post.

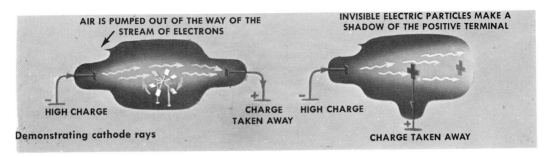

AIR IS PUMPED OUT OF THE WAY OF THE STREAM OF ELECTRONS

HIGH CHARGE   CHARGE TAKEN AWAY

Demonstrating cathode rays

INVISIBLE ELECTRIC PARTICLES MAKE A SHADOW OF THE POSITIVE TERMINAL

HIGH CHARGE   CHARGE TAKEN AWAY

In order to determine the nature of this phenomenon, he built a special low-pressure tube coated on the inside with chemicals that would glow when exposed to high voltage. Part way down the length of the tube was a round plate with a narrow slit in it so that the path of the beam could be studied. The experiment proved that the beam was bent or deflected toward the positive terminal. Since light cannot be deflected by charged plates, the theory of moving negatively charged particles emitting from the negative terminal (the CATHODE) was established. When Sir Joseph John Thomson, in the late 19th Century, wrote a summary about these negative particles of cathode rays, he called them *electrons*.   E. I. D.

Cathode-ray tube Cathode-ray tubes are ELECTRON beam tubes with a luminescent screen upon which the moving pattern of the beam can be seen. The cathode-ray tube may be one of two types: (1) The OSCILLOSCOPE, or oscillograph, used for graphical representation of electrical signals, and (2) the picture tube or kinescope, used for reproducing televised pictures. The physical appearance of both tubes is similar. Functionally, they differ by the number of luminous traces seen on the screen.

Three primary parts make up the tube:

1) *Envelope*—a glass or metal high-vacuum enclosure supporting the electron gun and phosphor screen. It may be for a 1" to 22" (2.54 to 55.88 cm.) diameter, round face; or for an 8" to 27" (20.32 to 65.58 cm.) diagonal, rectangular face.

2) *Electron gun*—located in the slim neck of the funnel. This component produces, focuses, and deflects the electron beam. The heated CATHODE "shoots" electrons through the control grid and accelerating grid. As the focused electron beam passes the deflection grids or coils, it is rapidly moved vertically and horizontally to produce a pattern on the screen.

3) *Phosphor screen*—the wide part of the envelope which holds the phosphor-coated glass. This illuminates when struck by bombarding electrons, producing the picture or graph.   E. I. D.

SEE ALSO: CATHODE RAY, ELECTRONICS, LUMINESCENCE, TELEVISION

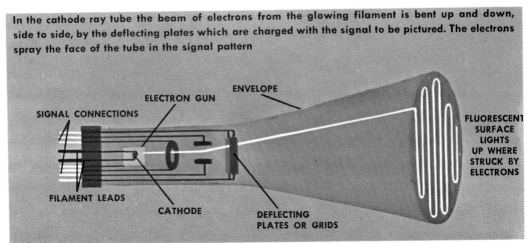

In the cathode ray tube the beam of electrons from the glowing filament is bent up and down, side to side, by the deflecting plates which are charged with the signal to be pictured. The electrons spray the face of the tube in the signal pattern

SIGNAL CONNECTIONS   ELECTRON GUN   ENVELOPE   FLUORESCENT SURFACE LIGHTS UP WHERE STRUCK BY ELECTRONS

FILAMENT LEADS   CATHODE   DEFLECTING PLATES OR GRIDS

Catkin A catkin is a long slender cluster of flowers on many woody plants.

Catkins flowers are all the same sex, either male or female. The male flowers of the birch, alder, and turkey oak are catkins. The fine catkin pollen is carried by wind and often contributes to people's allergies.   H.J.C.

Catnip Catnip, also called *catmint,* is a MINT plant that has a strong scent. Cats like this scent and cat toys use catnip leaves. Its heart-shaped leaves are a pale, gray-green.

Catnip plants grow from 2 to 3 feet (.61 to .91 meters) tall. Many tiny flowers cluster at the tip of the long stalks. The flowers are light violet or white.

Catnip can grow wild in North America, although it is originally from Europe. This PERENNIAL herb is sometimes raised in gardens. In some places its leaves are used to brew a medicinal tea.   M.R.L.

SEE ALSO: HERBS

Cattail Cattail, or *reed mace,* as it is called in England, is a wild plant which grows in marshy places. The narrow leaves will grow 3 to 6 feet (.91 to 1.83 meters) tall. The strong, straight flower stem grows 3 to 8 feet (.91 to 2.44 meters) tall. The dark brown clump of flowers looks like the end of a cat's tail.

A cattail seed has a parachute of down. Wind may disperse the seeds great distances. Cattail leaves were once used for weaving mats and seats of chairs. The entire plant is used as a winter bouquet.   J.K.K.

SEE ALSO: SEED DISPERSAL

Cattle see Artiodactyla, Cow, Oxen

Caucasoid see Evolution of Man

Cattails
Courtesy Society For Visual Education. Inc.

Cauliflower

Cauliflower (KAHL-ee-flower) Cauliflower is a variety of CABBAGE. The word *cauliflower* means "stemflower." It has a solid head of white flower clusters (the part that is eaten) which grow on top of a short stalk.

Cauliflower is difficult to raise and takes special care. It will grow only in cool, moist areas. Most gardeners buy rooted cauliflower plants. When the first button-like swelling appears on the stem, the outer leaves of the plant must be tied up loosely to shade the flower. The plant should be cut when the flower buds are fully formed but not yet opened.   M. R. L.

Caustic (KAW-stick) A caustic is a chemical substance which can burn or destroy living tissue. Caustics are alkalies (bases) used in industrial processes and in household cleaning products. The word "caustic" comes from the Greek word *kaustikos* which means "burning."

Cave A cave is a hollowed-out space in the earth. Cave formation begins along fracture lines and bedding planes where rocks such as *limestone* can be easily dissolved by *groundwater*. Given enough time, a complex system of narrow to wide tunnels and open chambers can develop in what was once solid rock. Most caves begin developing at or just below the water table, and many caves were once completely filled with water.

Mammoth Cave in Kentucky is huge. To explore all Mammoth Cave's rooms and passages, a person would travel about 200 miles (321.87 kilometers.) Some of the rooms are over 50 feet (15.24 meters) high. There are many streams and pools in Mammoth Cave. Visitors can travel in boats on some of these streams. Sightless fish live in this water. Because the cave is dark, the fish do not need eyes for seeing. In Mammoth

Cathedral Caverns, Alabama   A.H.I.A.

Cave is the never changing temperature of 54° F. (12.2° C.).

Carlsbad Caverns in New Mexico are probably the largest system of caves so far discovered. Other famous caves in the United States are the Wyandotte Cave in Indiana and the Wind Cave in South Dakota.

Unlike the caves formed by underground water, *sea caves* are carved in cliffs by pounding ocean waves. A fine example of a sea cave can be found at St. Martin's beach near St. John, New Brunswick, Canada.

Another type of cave is the *lava cave,* formed by the lava of a VOLCANO. The Singing Cave in Iceland is a lava cave.

When icebergs or glaciers melt and then freeze again, they form another kind of cave known as the *ice cave.* The Eisreisenwelt Cave in Austria is an example.

Caves have been very valuable to the scientist in his study of early man and of plant and animal life. Cave men lived in caves in southern France and northern Spain 100,000 years ago. The cave men left many paintings on the walls, showing the types of animals they hunted. By analyzing the floors of caves and ashes of fires, much of the cave man's life story has been pieced together. Many FOSSILS of early plant and animal life have been discovered in caves.

P.F.D.

SEE ALSO: ARCHEOLOGY, GEOLOGY, GLACIER

Caviar (KAH-vee-are) Caviar is the roe, or eggs, of a STURGEON found in the Black or Caspian seas. The eggs, salted and canned, are considered a table delicacy by many.

Cavity see Tooth decay

Cavy see Guinea pig

Cayenne (kye-YENN) Cayenne is a hot-tasting ground red PEPPER. It is used in highly flavored foods such as chili and tamales. Cayenne is made from the dried, ripe fruit of several kinds of *Capsicum* plants commonly called chilies or red peppers.   J.K.K.

SEE ALSO: PAPRIKA

Cedar (SEE-der) Cedars are evergreen trees. They belong to the PINE family. True cedars grow very slowly and become very tall. They have widespreading branches with leaves that look like green needles. Cones hang from the branches, and seeds are found under scales of the cones. Most people like the fresh, sweet, odor of cedar wood. This reddish-colored wood is very sturdy.

Cedar is a general term referring not only to those in genus *Cedrus,* but to other genera as well. The *cigarbox* or *Spanish cedar* has deciduous leaves and belongs to the *mahogany* family. The wood of this tropical tree repels insects.

Of the true cedars, the *incense cedar* grows over 150-feet (45.72 meters) tall and is found in several western states. In this same area, the hardest of all cedars, the *Port Orford,* is found. The *western red cedar,* 175 feet (53.34 meters) tall and 35 feet (10.67 meters) in diameter, is used for shingles and pilings. The *southern white cedar* is a smaller tree (80 feet or 24.38 meters) found in the Gulf states and along the Atlantic coast. The *eastern red cedar* has red heartwood and white sapwood. This cedar is an alternate host for apple RUST, a fungus that causes cedar leaves to form galls.   H.J.C.

Red cedar   Courtesy Society For Visual Education, Inc.

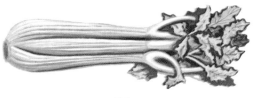

Celery

Celery Celery is a vegetable that may be eaten either raw or cooked. The stalks that are eaten are the stems of the leaves, called *petioles*. The "heart" is the short stem. Celery came from a wild, bitter HERB used centuries ago in medicines.

Celery, a member of the PARSLEY family, is raised in moist soil in California, Florida, Michigan, New York, and Colorado. It is blanched by using boards or special blanching paper to shut out the sun from the fleshy stalks. J. K. K.

Celestial navigation Celestial navigation is the science of determining position on earth with the use of heavenly bodies. During the daytime the sun is used for reference, and at night the stars, planets, and moon are used for reference.

Before the development of modern electronic navigation devices, celestial navigation was very important to ships at sea and to aircraft that were making transoceanic flights. It was particularly important in the days of sailing ships. One of the early instruments used in celestial navigation was the ASTROLABE.

The accuracy of precise celestial navigation is dependent upon several things: the training and skill of the navigator, the accuracy and type of instruments used, and the weather conditions at the time of the reading. Cloudy weather prevents precise celestial navigation.

The basic tools needed by the celestial navigator are: (1) a sextant, necessary for observing the angle of celestial bodies; (2) a chronometer, a special type of watch which has a second hand and keeps Greenwich Mean Time (GMT); (3) an *Air* or *Nautical Almanac,* which is used to locate the position of heavenly bodies for a given date of the year from different positions on earth, and (4) numerical tables, needed for computing the exact position. H. S. G.

SEE ALSO: NAVIGATION

Cellophane Cellophane is a material made from CELLULOSE, the chemical substance which lines the walls of plant cells. It is a tough, moisture-proof, gas-proof material, manufactured in various thicknesses and colors. A common use of cellophane is for packaging foods.

The first quantity production of cellophane occured in 1911 when J.E. Brandenburger designed a machine which made a continuous roll of the strong, transparent film. He named this product cellophane, a combination of the words, *cellulose* and *diaphane* (transparency).

Cellophane was formerly used as a package wrap. This job is now mainly done by plastic wraps. The compound used to make cellophane is now drawn into a fiber which is called *rayon.* V.B.I.

A sextant tells the altitude of a star. The altitude is the angle between two lines—one, from ship to star and, two, from ship to point on Earth directly below star. The exact position of the ship is calculated from readings from several stars

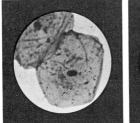

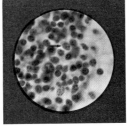

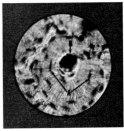

Cells from inside the cheek are thin, flat and arranged for smoothness and flexibility. (900 times magnification)

Red blood cells have no nuclei and do not reproduce themselves. A and B are white cells with nuclei. (500x)

Lymph cells (arrow) fight disease like white blood cells. Surrounding cells are of lymph gland. (1200x)

Bone cells (at A) make hardening chemicals. A blood vessel (B) and canals are also shown. (300x)

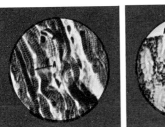

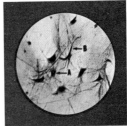

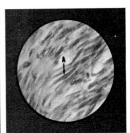

Photo-micrographs by National Teaching Aids, Inc.

Voluntary muscle cells look like striped ribbons. Long fibers within the cell contract. Nucleus is at A. (900x)

Gland cells in large intestine secrete digestive substances. A is a gland with duct. B is nucleus of the cell. (360x)

Nerve cells from the spinal cord. A is the cell body from which branches spread out. B is a blood vessel. (60x)

Involuntary muscles are not striped and are shorter than voluntary. A points to a good example. (900x)

Cells If a school building had only one big classroom, all of the boys and girls would have to work together. While some were trying to study, others would be listening to music or playing basketball. Schools have to be divided into separate rooms, so that people can do different things in different rooms.

Scientists used to think that the smallest part of a tree was its smallest leaf or root. When the microscope was invented, they discovered that all plants and animals, like school buildings, are really made up of tiny rooms, called *cells*. Each cell is surrounded by a thin skin or membrane, just as rooms are surrounded by walls.

Schools are built of many materials, such as brick, wood or steel. Plants and animals are built of one material, called *protoplasm*. This is the only living material known. Just as boys and girls are always moving from one room to the next, materials in protoplasm move from one cell to another. While students pass through doors, protoplasm moves through tiny openings in the membrane.

When plants and animals, like the blue-green ALGAE or the AMEBA, consist of one cell, that cell must do all of the work. When organisms are built of many cells, these cells are able to divide the work. All cells have personal housekeeping duties, such as taking in food and getting rid of waste products. Just as many doctors are specialists in blood disease or bone surgery, most cells are specialists in certain parts of the body. These specialized cells work in teams. Together, they form a *tissue*. The liver and intestine are examples of organs made up of many tissues.

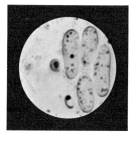

Bacteria are one-celled plants. Unlike most cells, bacteria have no nuclei. (1500x)

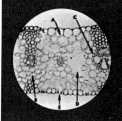

Parts of a leaf: A—clear cell; B—nucleus; C—vein; D—air space; E—breathing pore. (300x)

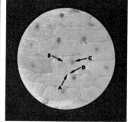

Photo-micrographs by National Teaching Aids, Inc.

Dead cork cells have no inner material. Hooke discovered cells from cork. (300x)

Stained onion skin shows A—cell wall, B—cytoplasm, C—nucleus, D—membrane. (200x)

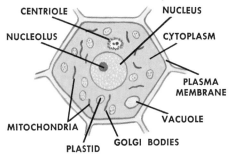

CENTRIOLE   NUCLEUS

NUCLEOLUS   CYTOPLASM

PLASMA MEMBRANE

MITOCHONDRIA   VACUOLE

PLASTID   GOLGI BODIES

A diagrammatic generalized cell

Protoplasm is a mixture of chemicals. Carbon, hydrogen, oxygen, and nitrogen are the main elements in protoplasm. Molecules of these are put together to form ORGANIC COMPOUNDS—carbohydrates, fats, and proteins, as well as inorganic compounds—water and minerals. Since the molecules are constantly reacting with one another, protoplasm is always in a chemical turmoil. The molecules around the outside of the cell form a skin called the *plasma membrane.* Tiny pores in the membrane are gateways through which molecules may pass. However, the membrane is very selective. It accepts or rejects molecules as they are needed by the cell.

The cell consists of a *nucleus,* which is surrounded by *cytoplasm* (cell plasm). The nucleus is like the teacher in the classroom, since it is responsible for the main activities of the cell. It is a large jelly-like mass usually surrounded by another membrane. It is a house for the CHROMOSOMES, the carriers of GENES. The nucleus also has its own small nucleus called the *nucleolus.*

Within the cytoplasm, many small granules, rods, and droplets are suspended. Although these have been given various names, scientists are not positive of their individual functions. Rounded bodies, called *mitochondria,* are respiratory sites for furnishing energy to the cell. The tiny granules, called *microsomes,* are probably the chief centers for the putting together of proteins. *Golgi bodies,* which look like fine mesh, are probably responsible for the manufacture of secretion products, since many are found in cells of glands. Oval bodies, called PLASTIDS, are found in plant cells. These may contain pigment or coloring matter. When they are green, they contain CHLOROPHYLL and are centers for PHOTOSYNTHESIS. A tiny body, called a *centriole,* is located just outside the nucleus. Occurring in animal cells and in some plant cells, it functions during cell reproduction.

Cytoplasm also contains much unabsorbed food which is found either in granules or *vacuoles.* Vacuoles are small spaces filled with solids, liquids, or gases and surrounded by a membrane. They may be filled with raw food or waste material. They may be centers for storage of starch, fat, or water.

Certain types of cells may have an extra wall surrounding the plasma membrane. Since plants need protection and support against gravity, plant cells have rigid, CELLULOSE walls. While animal cells do not have true cell walls, often the outer layer of cells secretes a thick covering such as the CHITIN, found in arthropods.

Cells produce new cells by dividing. Since new cells can arise only from existing cells, all life is continuous. All living cells of today have come from ancestor cells which existed billions of years ago.   E. P. L.
SEE ALSO: MITOSIS AND MEIOSIS, NERVE CELL, PLANT TISSUE, PROTOZOA

Cells, in series and parallel see Battery, Electricity

Celluloid Celluloid was the first synthetic plastic. It was made from CELLULOSE. It was developed by John W. Hyatt in 1863 as a substitute for ivory billiard balls. It is now used in combs and brush handles.   A.J.H.

Cellulose (SELL-yuh-lohs) The paper in this book is made almost entirely of cellulose. The cell walls of green plants contain this material. It is a complex CARBOHYDRATE.

Cotton and flax fibers are almost pure cellulose. The long, strong fibers of spruce supply one-third of the wood pulp used in PAPER. The kind of paper manufactured depends upon the nature and treatment of cellulose. Chemically it is a POLYMER of glucose, with formula $(C_6H_{10}O_5)_x$.

Celluloid was the first cellulose plastic. *Cellophane* and *rayon* were created in the 1910's. *Cellulose nitrate* is made into explosives, artificial fabrics, as oil cloth and leather substitutes, and varnishes.   H.J.C.

Concrete mixer

Cement Cement is a soft gray powder that is made from lime, silica and alumina. It is mixed with water and sand to make mortar. This material will hold bricks together in buildings. Concrete is a mixture of cement, sand, gravel and water, and it is used in making pavements and sidewalks. It is also very useful in building dams, bridges, and canal locks.

About two-thirds of the material used in making cement is lime which comes from limestone and various shells. These rock-like substances are crushed and ground up in huge machines. This material is then dried and ground again before it goes to the kiln for roasting. This process gives it its binding properties. The final step is the addition of a small amount of GYPSUM and a final grinding to powder.   D. E. Z.

Celsius see Centigrade

Cenozoic Era (see-nuh-ZO-ick) The Cenozoic Era is the present period of geologic time. It represents the most recent history of the earth. Referred to as the *Age of Mammals,* it covers a period of time of at least 65 million years. Nearly all of the important features of the earth's surface today were formed during this era.

TERTIARY PERIOD

The era is divided into two periods and six epochs, listed from oldest to youngest. The *Tertiary* period extended from 65 million to one million years ago. The ocean covered the southeastern United States. The Sierra Nevadas (United States), the Alps (Europe), and the Himalayas (Asia) were formed. There were many volcanoes.

FOSSILS of the major plant groups are found in the Tertiary rock layers. As the climate grew cooler and drier, grasses replaced the forests. Only those plants that shed leaves to live through the cold survived in the northern regions.

One-celled, coin-shaped protozoans (nummulites) were abundant in the seas. Their shells helped make thick limestone formations. Mammals lived all over the world. Bones and teeth found in the sediment layers show the changes in animal forms for each successive epoch. Most of the world's oil and many metals are found in these rock layers.

The *Paleocene* epoch is the oldest division of the Tertiary period. The climate was wet and semi-tropical. The paleocene rocks were sandstone, shale and low grade coal. The mammals were small and unspecialized.

The *Eocene* was an epoch of expanding seas and large lakes. South America was separate from North America. New animals appeared. There were blunt-toothed, dull-witted mammals (creodonts), the first horses (Eohippus) and small ancestors of the deer, pig and camel. Rabbits, moles, insects, monkeys, bats and whales existed at this time. Eocene is often classed with Paleocene as one epoch.

The *Oligocene,* middle Tertiary epoch, was marked by volcanoes and floods. Fossils found in the sand and silt of the White River beds indicate that the animals in North America forty million years ago resembled

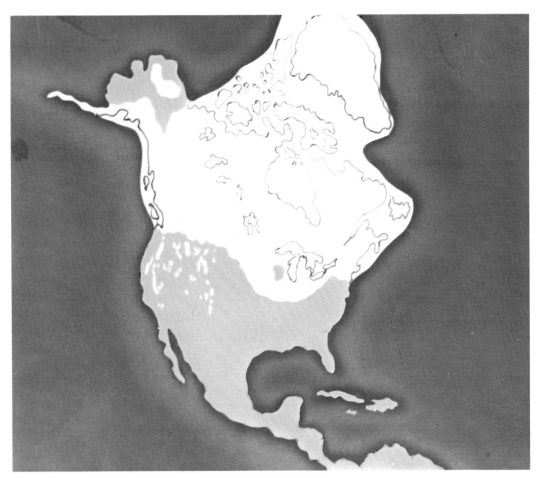

Huge glaciers covered much of North America during the Pleistocene epoch of the Cenozoic Era. They left the terrain much as it is today

those of central Africa today.

The *Miocene* epoch, the high point of mammal life, developed the MASTODON, panther, bear, weasel, skunk, sloth and the armadillo. The Alps and Himalaya mountains were formed. There were probably land links between Asia and North America, and between Africa and Europe. Florida emerged.

The *Pliocene,* or last Tertiary epoch, was drier and cooler. The mammals of the warm climates were extinct or lived near the Equator.

QUATERNARY PERIOD

The Quaternary period is the most recent time span of less than a million years.

The *Pleistocene* epoch is the ice age and the age of man. Huge glaciers, thousands of feet thick, like those of Antarctica and Greenland covered Northern Europe and North America as far south as the Ohio River. Dried and frozen skeletons of great mammals have been found: MAMMOTHS, beavers as large as bears, and wolves as tall

as man. It is certain that man developed during this time.

Sediments and fossils indicate that extensive glaciers were followed by warmer climates when the ice sheet slowly melted, leaving fresh water lakes. Winds blew fine rock over the great plains forming its fertile soil. Sand piled up in dunes.

Four glacial and three interglacial stages have been charted. Cores of sediment brought up from the ocean beds indicate there may have been from five to fifteen cold-warm cycles. Time estimates for the ice age vary from 280,000 years to 800,000 years.

The last great continental ice sheet, called the Wisconsin Age, retreated from the North American continent about 11,000 years ago. Our present period of the Cenozoic Era is called the *Recent Epoch.* Most geologists feel the earth is in an *Ice Age* cycle, and say that a continental ice sheet will again form. A.P.M.
SEE ALSO: EVOLUTION OF MAN, GEOLOGIC TIME TABLE, GLACIAL AGES, PALEONTOLOGY

Centaurus (senn-TAW-rus) Centaurus, or the Centaur, is a CONSTELLATION that can be seen from the southern part of the earth. It is famous because its brightest star, *Alpha Centauri,* is the closest star to the earth visible to the eye.

Alpha Centauri is one of the 20 brightest stars. It is only about 4 light years away from the earth, or about 25 trillion miles (40 trillion kilometers). Another one of Centaurus's stars, *Proxima Centauri,* is even closer to the earth than Alpha Centauri. Proxima Centauri is a very faint star. It can be seen only with a telescope.

Beta Centauri, Centaurus's second brightest star, is also one of the twenty brightest stars. Alpha and Beta Centauri are sometimes called the *Southern Pointers* because they point to another famous southern hemisphere constellation, the Southern Cross. Alpha Centauri is a beautiful yellow star. Beta Centauri is blue-white.

The stars and constellations of the southern hemisphere were first noticed and named during the Middle Ages, when adventurers began to explore the southern and western world.

In July and August, people in southern Florida and Texas can sometimes see Centaurus. In the early evening during those months it would be very low on the horizon in the extreme south of the United States.

C. L. K.

SEE ALSO: ALPHA, CRUX

Centaurus, the Centaur

Centigrade or Celsius This is a scale for measuring temperature based on the boiling point and freezing point of water. The freezing point of water is 0° Celsius. The boiling point of water is 100° Celsius.

The Celsius scale is divided into 100 equal divisions. This is the scale most often used in the science laboratory and in most countries.

This scale was established by a Swedish astronomer, Anders Celsius (1701-1744). As first presented by Celsius, the scale had the freezing point of water at 100° and the boiling point at 0°. This was quickly reversed.

A.J.H.

SEE ALSO: TEMPERATURE SCALES

Centipede

Centipede The centipede is a small animal with many legs. It is related to the MILLIPEDE but is in a class by itself, *Chilopoda.* Centipedes are hunters, feeding on small animals that live in or on the soil. They kill prey with poison from special claws on the first pair of legs.

Most American centipedes are 1 to 2 inches (2.54 to 5.08 centimeters) long. Tropical species are 6 inches to 1 foot (15.24 to 30.48 centimeters) long. There are about 3,000 to 5,000 species of chilopods in four orders. Antennae are threadlike. The first body segment bears a pair of curved poison claws. Behind it are 15 to 18 leg-bearing segments, the most in tropical species. The last two segments lack legs and are for reproduction. Legs get progressively longer from anterior to posterior. Young have four pairs of legs and molt six times. About two leg segments are added each time the centipede molts.

J.C.K.

SEE ALSO: ANTHROPODA, MILLIPEDE

WHAT IS CENTRIFUGAL FORCE?

1   Fill a pail one-third full of water. Swing it quickly up over your head and down in a circular fashion. The water clings to the bottom of the pail and does not spill out.

2   Put an inch of water in a round vase. Turn it rapidly sidewise. The water will leave the bottom and cling to the round sides.   1″ = 2.5 cm.

3   Centrifugal force keeps an object moving in a circle the farthest away from the center of revolution.

Centrifugal and centripetal forces If a ball is whirled at the end of a string in a circular motion, it would seem as if the ball were suddenly very heavy and were pulling harder as it is whirled faster. The force of the string pulling the ball toward the center of the circle is the *centripetal force*. The force seeming to act on the string by the ball is the *centrifugal force*.

An apparent outward force on an object rotating about an axis is met with an equal inward force in order to continue the rotation. The outward force is centrifugal and the inward force is centripetal. This phenomenon is an example of Sir Isaac Newton's third law of motion: "Every force is accompanied by an equal and opposite reacting force."

The reaction of the centripetal force is the result of the ball's tending to continue on a path tangent to the circle. The string keeps pulling the ball in, to keep it in a circular

CAN ONE INCREASE CENTRIFUGAL FORCE?

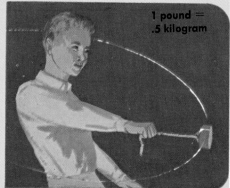

1 pound = .5 kilogram

1   Fasten a one pound weight to the end of a strong string. Holding the other end of the string, start swinging the weight in a circle. Swing it as fast as possible. Feel the pull on the arm.

2   Replace the small weight with a heavier one. Repeat the circular motion. Is the pull on the arm greater?

3   Centrifugal force is the pull of an object which is moving in a circle. Increasing the weight and speed of the moving object will increase the centrifugal force. Centripetal force is exerted by the arm to keep the object from flying out. This is the equal and opposite of centrifugal force.

motion, instead of allowing it to go straight —on the tangent. When the string is released, the ball does not fly straight out as centrifugal force would indicate, nor does the ball pull in toward the center as centripetal force suggests. Releasing the string eliminates the centripetal force since there is no force pulling the ball inward. At the same time, the equal and opposite reaction, centrifugal force, which is actually the pull of the string on the center axis, also disappears.

The CENTRIFUGE is a device which uses the principle of centrifugal force for separating liquids or liquids and solids into the individual components. The separation of cream from milk, and water from laundry illustrates this. Engines are sometimes equipped with centrifugal governors to control their speed. As rotating weights move outward, the attached linkage changes the setting of the engine's throttle.   E. I. D.

SEE ALSO: NEWTON, SIR ISAAC

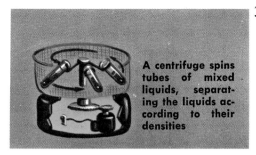

A centrifuge spins tubes of mixed liquids, separating the liquids according to their densities

From ground-hugging leaves, the famous century plant sends blossoms high in the air

Courtesy Society For
Visual Education, Inc.

Centrifuge (SENN-truh-fewj) A centrifuge is a rotating machine having a hollow rotor. A mixture of liquids, or solids and liquids may be fed into it and then subjected to high speeds and centrifugal force, so that the mixture will be separated into its component parts (because of the difference in densities of the components).

The centrifuge is used to separate cream from milk. A centrifugal separator can separate particles from smoke. The isotope uranium-235 is separated from the other isotopes of uranium by a high-speed centrifuge. In the space program, astronauts were subjected to great forces in a very large centrifuge to test their reactions. In medical laboratories body fluid specimens are centrifuged to separate cells and other components for study.   D.L.D./A.J.H.

Centriole see Cells

Centripetal see Centrifugal and centripetal forces

Century plant It once was thought that this plant took a century (100 years) to bloom. It actually flowers in about 20 years and then dies. It is a member of the *amaryllis family* native to Mexico.

The thick leaves form a rosette or group of circles near the ground. Each leaf may be 6 inches (15.24 centimeters) wide and 6 feet (1.83 meters) long. A flower stalk rises above the leaves for 30 feet (9.14 meters). The yellow flowers form a panicle and look somewhat like lilies.

SISAL fibers from the large leaves are used commercially. The sap of the plant is distilled in Mexico to make an alcoholic drink called *mescal*. Botanically, the century plant is called *Agave americana*.   H.J.C.

Cepheus (SEE-fyoos) Cepheus is a group of stars that looks like a triangle on top of a square. It is not a very bright CONSTELLATION, but in the northern part of the world it can be seen on almost any clear night. It is near POLARIS, the bright star in the Dipper.

Cepheus was the name of an ancient king of Ethiopia. Cepheus; his wife, CASSIOPEIA; their daughter, Andromeda; and Perseus are a group of constellations known as the Royal Family. The Greeks believed that Cepheus was one of the men called Argonauts who went with Jason to find the Golden Fleece. In another legend, Cepheus had to offer his daughter Andromeda as a sacrifice to a sea monster because Cassiopeia had boasted that she was more beautiful than the sea nymphs. Perseus rescued Andromeda.

Some of the stars in the Cepheus constellation are "variable" stars, which means that their brightness varies. Delta, the fourth brightest star of the group, is especially variable. Stars of this type are called "Cepheid variables." There is a rhythmical pattern of change in brightness which astronomers can study and determine the true brightness of the star.   C. L. K.

Cepheus

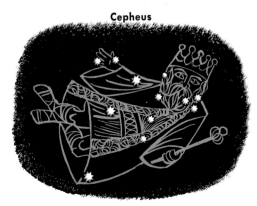

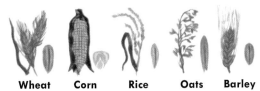

Wheat Corn Rice Oats Barley

Cereal grains They belong to the grass family. There are six true cereal grains: CORN, WHEAT, OATS, BARLEY, RICE, and RYE. Their stems are hollow and jointed. The leaves are long and slender. The fruit or grain has one seed.

Cereal grains have an extensive fibrous root system. The leaves have parallel veins and are alternate on the culm or stem. The flower is an inflorescence called a spikelet. It is wind pollinated. One stalk of corn can produce up to 50 million pollen grains. The ovary matures into a dry indehiscent FRUIT called a caryopsis. The seeds are low in water, so they can be easily stored. They are high in food value, containing carbohydrates, protein, some fats, and vitamins. They are the most important, economically, of all the monocots.

Wheat and corn are annuals grown in the temperate regions. Rice is a tropical grain. These three are the major cereals in production and consumption. They belong to the family Gramineae. H. J. C.

Cerebellum (sehr-uh-BELL-uhm) The cerebellum is part of the brain. It is located below and at the base of the cerebrum and is part of the hindbrain. The other part of the hindbrain is called the brain stem. It is composed of medulla, pons, and midbrain. The cerebellum connects to the brain stem by three large bundles of fibers called *peduncles*. The two outer lobes of the cerebellum are connected by a middle part called the *vermis*. The cerebellum coordinates voluntary skeletal muscle.

The cerebellum is located beneath and behind the main part of the brain

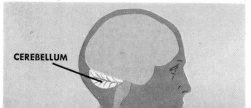

CEREBELLUM

The cerebellar surface appears layered because it is crossed by parallel fissures and *sulci* (grooves). Fissures are deeper grooves than sulci.

The outer layer is called gray matter since it is composed mainly of cell bodies of nerve fibers. Among its cells are the large branching Purkinje cells, found no other place in the nervous system. White matter, composed of sheathed fibers, is deeper in the cerebellum. These fibers branch out, appearing treelike in section. This relationship between gray and white matter is opposite to that in the spinal cord.

Since the cerebellum regulates muscular activity, it is involved in walking, sitting, standing, and skilled movement. It works with the semicircular canals in the inner ear to maintain equilibrium and balance. J. C. K.
SEE ALSO: NERVOUS SYSTEM

Cerebral palsy (SER-uh-bruhl-PALL-zee) Cerebral palsy is a disease which starts at or even before birth. About one or two babies out of every 1000 are affected. The usual causes are a defect in the development of the BRAIN (CEREBRUM), a break-down of brain cells while they are being formed, or an injury before or at birth.

Premature infants are occasionally found to be born with normal head size and intelligence, but weakness and partial paralysis of the lower legs are noted after a few months. In other cases, full-term infants whose brains are deprived of blood supply (and therefore oxygen) during difficult labors are born limp, unable to suck, and needing oxygen to begin breathing. These children will not only be severely weak physically, but will also have complete retardation of development and thinking. Other babies are born with lack of blood flow to just one area of the brain, causing muscular problems, especially in the legs, which are noted when the child tries to stand or walk. The classic cross-leg or "scissors gait" walk of cerebral palsy is due to weakness of certain leg muscles, causing the person to walk on tip-toe with toes pointed inward.

If children having cerebral palsy can be diagnosed at an early age, special exercises and treatments can allow many of them to develop their full learning abilities. E.S.S.

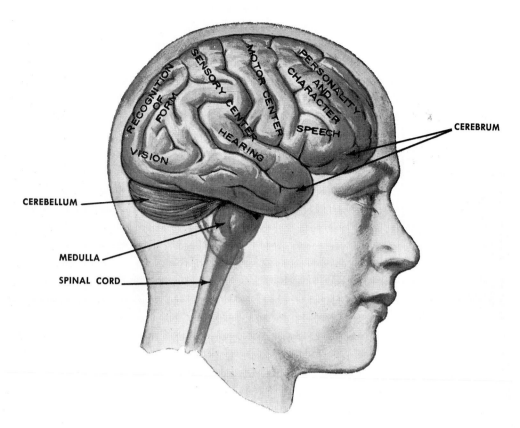

Labels on image: RECOGNITION OF FORM, SENSORY CENTER, MOTOR CENTER, PERSONALITY AND CHARACTER, HEARING, SPEECH, VISION, CEREBRUM, CEREBELLUM, MEDULLA, SPINAL CORD

TODAY'S HEALTH, published by AMERICAN MEDICAL ASSOCIATION

Cerebrum (Ser-REE-brum) The cerebrum is the largest or main part of the BRAIN. The cerebrum controls the ability to think. Man is probably the only animal that has this ability. Each part of the cerebrum has a duty to perform. One part controls imagination and memory. Other parts control the senses of smell, taste, touch, hearing, sight and speech. One area controls purposeful movement of the muscles. This makes it possible for a person to throw a ball, dance, or jump rope at a selected time.

The cerebrum is like a switchboard. The switchboard receives the dial tones, and soon telephones in far away places ring. The cerebrum receives the impulses and directs the body into action. The impulses travelling the nerve cells are the messengers to and from the cerebrum.

The cerebrum has many ridges and indentations. Each person has a cerebrum of a different design just as each person has a different fingerprint or handwriting. If the cerebrum is injured in one area the functions or the sense that the injured area controls may be impaired.

The cerebrum is composed of gray and white matter. The gray matter is on the surface in what is called the *cortex*. The gray matter consists of large masses of nerve cells. The nerve cells are interlaced and connected in endless ways. The cerebrum is partially divided into right and left hemispheres by a cleft, the longitudinal fissure. Each hemisphere has four lobes, the frontal, parietal, occipital and temporal. The *frontal* lobe controls muscular activity. The *parietal* lobe is the center for pressure, pain and temperature responses. The *occipital* is concerned with sight, and the *temporal* area receives impulses from the tongue, nose, and ears. There are nerves that connect each lobe with every other part of the brain. There are many combinations of nerve fibers. Fibers from one hemisphere cross to the opposite side at various levels. If the right side of the cerebrum is injured, the left side may be affected. M. I. L.

SEE ALSO: NERVOUS SYSTEM

Greenland whale

Dolphin

Cereus, night-blooming see Night-blooming plants

Cerium (SEER-ee-uhm) Cerium (symbol Ce) is a RARE EARTH ELEMENT number 58 in Mendeleev's Periodic Table. Cerium oxide (CeO_2) polishes eyeglasses.

Cerium has an *atomic mass number* (*atomic weight*) of 140.12. Its *oxidation numbers* (VALENCE) are $+3$ and $+4$. The $+4$ *ion* allows cerium to separate from other rare earths. Cerium magnesium nitrate, a *para magnetic* SALT, is used for TEMPERATURE SCALE studies by nuclear orientation near ABSOLUTE ZERO. Bombarded $^{140}_{58}Ce$ is used to explain rapidly rotating *nuclei*. J. Berzelius and W. Hisinger (and M. Klaproth independently) discovered cerium in 1803.

M. S. P.

Cesium (SEE-zee-uhm) Cesium is a shiny, whitish ELEMENT. It is one of the *alkali* metals which, like SODIUM, react quickly with water. It must be stored under oil.

Robert Bunsen and Gustav Kirchhoff discovered cesium in 1860 in German spring water. It has since been mined with deposits of lepidolite and monazite.

Its main uses are in the removal of oxygen from electronic tubes and as an organic hydrogenation catalyst.

Cesium (symbol Cs) has atomic number 55. Its atomic weight is 132.905.   D.A.B.

Cetacea (sih-TAY-shuh) Cetacea is the order of mammals that includes WHALES and PORPOISES. Like all mammals, they are warm blooded, breathe air, and have skin. Cetaceans differ from most mammals because they live only in the water, have no hind limbs, and have no connection between the nose and mouth.

All have paddle-like *flippers* for forelimbs and swim by using their *flukes* (horizontally flattened tails). They also have a layer of fat called *blubber* just under their skin and have a nose opening, *blowhole,* on top of their heads.

Cetaceans live in salt water, and many migrate great distances. They are seldom found in tropical waters although they go to warm water to bear young.

The three groups of Cetacea are the *whalebone whales* (such as the Greenland whale), the *toothed whales* (such as the dolphin and sperm whales) and the *fossil whales.*

A few of the aquatic adaptations of cetaceans are: (1) blubber which serves as stored food, as a heat insulator, and as a protection against increased water pressure at great depths; (2) more blood for their size than any other mammal; (3) ribs flexibly attached to the sternum for great chest expansion; (4) no upper vertebral processes for vertical tail flexibility. J. K. L.

Chain reaction A chain reaction is a series of molecular or atomic changes of a substance, in which, once the series is started, each change causes (sets off) the next one. The products of the first change affect the now-altered substance and cause a second change in which energy or other products are again released, and they in turn cause a third change in the constitution of the substance. This reaction may go on until some desired goal is reached.

SEE: NUCLEAR SCIENCE, NUCLEAR SCIENCE GLOSSARY

Chalcedony see Quartz

CHALK (WHITE) LIMESTONE

Chalk magnified to show types of crustaceans that form this soft, porous limestone
Courtesy Society For Visual Education, Inc.

Chalk Chalk is a type of limestone that is very soft and fine-grained. It is made up of the broken-down shells of microscopic one-celled sea animals. Chalk is the softest and most porous of all of the different types of limestones. Its color is usually white; however, it may range from buff or gray due to certain impurities found in it.

As the shells of millions of marine animals accumulated on shallow sea floors over great periods of time, chalk deposits resulted. Fossils of these animals are often found in these deposits. In the past, chalk was used as blackboard chalk, but today other materials are used. The famous white 'cliffs of Dover, England, are chalk cliffs.   H. S. G.

Chameleon (kuh-MEE-lee-un) The true chameleon is an Old World LIZARD belonging to the chameleon family. These lizards have long, extensible tongues that dart out with lightning speed to capture insects on their sticky ends.

The American or false chameleon belongs in the iguana family. This is the lizard sold at fairs. It changes color from brown to green.

Both the tail and feet are modified into grasping organs. Its eyes are mounted on stalks and can be focused independently. Its body is spiny with a boxlike head. It changes color, varying from slate gray to yellow to green. In the dark it is yellow. In light, on a dark background, it is gray. Both skin structure and nervous control bring about this change.

Its most striking characteristic is a throat fan. These are used in defense of territory and during courtship of the female. The fan is supported by a cartilage rod. When it flares out, scales separate and a brilliant color appears. These lizards have pads on their toes for climbing. Their tails are not *prehensile* (grasping). They feed on insects and spiders.

J. C. K.

SEE ALSO: LIZARD, REPTILIA

Changes of state see Physical states and changes; Substances, properties of

Channel The channel or bed of a river is the part that is actually covered by water. The *riverbanks* are the land running alongside the river and just above it. The word channel is also used to refer to the deepest part of a river, harbor, or strait. The channel is often marked in some manner to aid navigation.

The channel of a river is always in a state of constant change. In the stage of youth, a river channel is quite straight. As the river moves through maturity to old age, its channel becomes very uneven. In the stage of old age, a part of the original channel is often cut off from the main part of the channel as the river cuts a new course through a bend in the channel.   H. S. G.

Chaparral (SHAP-uh-rel) Chaparrals are one of the BIOMES of the world. These areas develop where the winters are not too cold but the summers are hot and dry.

The dense vegetation of small trees and shrubs usually doesn't exceed 8 feet (2½ meters). Quail, bobcats, condors, and mule deer live here. Chaparrals are often hit by fires. Some seeds need an annual burn or a high temperature for germination.   H.J.C.

369

HOW TO MAKE CHARCOAL

Materials: coffee can, hardwood, bunsen burner or stove

1 This should be done only when an older person is helping.
2 Puncture a hole in the lid of a coffee can. Place several small sticks of hardwood in the can. Replace the lid.
3 Heat the can over a bunsen burner or other heat source to drive out the water vapor in the wood.
4 As wood gas escapes from the hole light a match to it until the gas is all burned up. Remove the can from the heat and allow to cool.
5 The sticks of wood are now charcoal.

Charcoal Charcoal is a form of carbon made either from wood or the bones of animals. Charcoal is made by heating the material strongly without a good supply of air.

The process of making charcoal is called *destructive distillation.* In wood, many vapors are driven off and the black, porous residue is charcoal. The many air spaces allow charcoal to absorb many gases and coloring matter. Another form of carbon, *lampblack,* a very pure form, is made from natural gas and a variety of oils. It is used in printers' ink and shoe polish. Wood charcoal is a good fuel.   J. H. D.

Chard see Swiss chard

Charge see Battery, Electricity

Charged particles Charged particles are the tiny building blocks of atoms. They appear whenever atoms are disturbed. Stars constantly shoot charged particles through space. Streams of charged particles are called *rays,* or RADIATION.

These atomic parts are identified by their position in the atom, and by their size, weight, and behavior. Behavior partly depends on how these are charged. Some particles electrically attract each other; others repel. Of two attracting particles, one is positive and the other is negative. Particles of the same charge repel one another. Particles with no electrical attraction are called neutral.

The basic particles of an atom are *electrons* (negatively charged), *protons* (positively charged), and *neutrons* (neutral, or no charge).

There are other particles whose size and changeability make identification difficult. These subatomic particles include positrons, antiprotons, mesons, and neutrinos.

Still others, actual nuclei of certain atoms, also are called particles. One is the alpha particle (helium nucleus). Others are deutrons and tritons. Scientists are discovering more.

Machines called ACCELERATORS, or "atom smashers," isolate and use charged particles. They direct and accelerate the particles to bombard nuclei. Both alpha particles and protons are used.   D. J. I.
SEE ALSO: ATOM, NUCLEAR ENERGY

Charioteer see Auriga

Charles' Law Charles' Law is a statement concerning the action of a GAS or vapor in relation to its temperature and volume.

The *kinetic theory* of gases assumes that all gases are made up of tiny particles called MOLECULES. These molecules are very small compared to the distance which separates one particle from another. Since these molecules are in a constant state of motion, they bump into, or collide, with one another and also with the walls of the container which holds a gas. Because they are constantly moving about, each molecule has a certain amount of energy and this amount is about the same for each.

If the temperature of the gas is increased, the energy of each of the particles is also increased and they begin to move faster. If the volume of the container remains the same, the increased speed of their movement causes them to collide with the walls of the container more often and the pressure is increased. However, if the pressure is to remain the same as before, the volume containing the gas must be increased as the temperature is increased.

Hence, Charles' Law states: the volume of a gas at a constant pressure varies directly with the absolute temperature.   A. E. L.

Chat Chat is a name given to several species of birds of the WARBLER family. The yellow-breasted chat and long-tailed chat are found in the United States.

Arthur A. Allen

Yellow-breasted chat

Cheese see Dairy products

Cheetah see Cat family

Chemical change Chemical change is a re-arranging of ATOMS to form different kinds of materials. Energy of some sort such as heat usually is present when these changes come about. There are examples of chemical change in iron becoming rust, in burning fuels changing to smoke and ashes, and in dry cells producing ELECTRICITY. Chemical changes are constantly going on around and in man. They enable the body to use oxygen breathed and the food eaten. Plants make food through chemical change. Life would not continue without these important processes.

MAKING NEW MATERIALS FROM OLD

A chemical change occurs when materials are combined to make a product which has entirely different properties than the original materials.

1   Heat a slice of bread in a toaster or oven until it is black. It has changed to charcoal.

2   Mix two tablespoons of vinegar in a cup of milk. It forms curds.

3   Rub egg over a silver spoon. After an hour it will become tarnished.

or

Cover a silver coin with sulfur till the coin is black. Sulfur and silver combine to form silver sulfide.

4   Put iron filings in a jar. Sprinkle them with water. In the presence of moisture iron combines with oxygen to form rust.

5   Heat sugar until it is brown and turns to carmel.

6   Combine water, iron sulfate, and tannic acid to make ink.

In chemical change, the *electron* arrangement of the atom or molecule is altered, *not the nucleus* as in nuclear reactions. During chemical change, electrons in the atoms are borrowed, lent, or shared. These electrons seem to interact between pairs of atoms to form *chemical bonds* which hold these atoms together. The atoms as ions are chemically active, some moreso than others.

Some changes in appearance are merely physical changes. Physical change usually accompanies chemical change, while chemical change doesn't necessarily accompany physical change. For example, if a rock is ground into dust, the physical appearance is changed but not the chemical nature of the atoms of the rock. The dust is merely fine pieces of rock; likewise, when sawing a board in two, one has simply sliced between atoms and not through them. When electrons are borrowed or lent, *ionic* bonds are formed. When electrons are shared, the bonds formed are called *covalent* bonds. A material changed chemically cannot be returned to the original form by simple mechanical means.

As stated, heat, light or electrical ENERGY accompany any chemical change. When some materials combine they release heat. Cheap, abundant materials which do this are used as fuels. (NUCLEAR REACTORS also produce heat, but this represents nuclear, not chemical change.)

Whenever a chemical change occurs, it is always accompanied by an ENERGY change at the same time. This means that energy may either be taken in from, or may be given up to the surroundings. The energy may take the form of heat, electrical energy, light, or mechanical work. When a chemical process gives up energy, it is called an *exothermic* process. When the change results in absorption from the surroundings, it is an *endothermic* process. The burning of coal, gas, or oil to produce heat and other energy, or the operation of a flashlight battery to deliver electrical energy are examples of exothermic changes.

Photosynthesis and photography are examples of endothermic changes. In these, light energy is absorbed to cause the chemical reaction.

Many chemical changes will often occur so slowly, however, that the energy change, though present, may be hard to observe.

Chemists classify chemical changes into four groups. One type, for instance, is illustrated by the burning of coal. Coal is primarily made of carbon. Carbon atoms combine with oxygen atoms to form compounds of carbon monoxide or carbon dioxide.

An equation or "chemical sentence" which describes briefly what happens in a chemical reaction, uses symbols or abbreviations for the materials involved. An equation showing the above carbon reaction is $2C + O_2 \rightarrow 2CO$. This type of change is called *combination*.

A second class of chemical change can be illustrated in the breakdown of water molecules. A process called ELECTROLYSIS, using electricity to promote the change, breaks down water molecules to produce oxygen and hydrogen gases. An equation showing this reaction is $2H_2O \rightarrow 2H + O_2$. This type of reaction is *decomposition*.

A third kind of chemical change takes place when an atom or molecule replaces another in a compound solution such as copper sulfate. The iron changes place with the copper, and the copper which is set free can be seen. The equation showing this is Fe (iron) + $CuSO_4$ (copper sulfate) → $FeSO_4$ + Cu. This type is *replacement*.

In the fourth type, two compounds break down to exchange their parts. This happens for example when sodium chloride (table salt) and silver nitrate react, forming silver chloride and sodium nitrate. $NaCl + AgNO_3 \rightarrow AgCl + NaNO_3$. This is called a *double replacement* reaction.

All nature is involved in a maze of chemical reactions. C. F. R.

SEE ALSO: CHEMISTRY, HEAT OF REACTION, NUCLEAR SCIENCE

Chemical laws see Chemistry

Chemical warfare Chemical warfare is the military use of chemicals. These chemicals produce gas, fire, and smoke screens to injure or confuse people. Soldiers are trained to use gas masks and other devices to protect themselves against chemical warfare.

Chemical warfare dates back to 429 B.C., when the Spartans of Greece tried to suffocate their enemies by burning wood, pitch, and sulfur. However, rain put out the fire. A few years later the Spartans drove back their enemies by producing fumes of

ANCIENT SPARTAN
LAYING SMOKE SCREEN

WORLD WAR I
GAS MASK

WORLD WAR II
SMOKE SCREEN

boiling pitch, charcoal, and sulfur.

In 1915 the Germans used CHLORINE gas against the French and English troops, thus opening the era of modern chemical warfare. Later in World War I both the Allied Forces and the Germans made extensive use of gas warfare. Mustard gas, which caused slow-healing burns, was responsible for the greatest number of chemical warfare casualties in World War I.

Both the Allied and other powers of World War II maintained huge stockpiles of gas weapons. Since each side feared reprisals, no attempt was made to use the gas.

In World War II chemical smoke screens were used on the battlefields and seas. These smoke screens hid the movement of troops and ships and were effective in landing actions. Smoke was beneficial in blinding and confusing the enemy. Colored smoke was employed for signals.

Fire was used in many forms during World War II. Attacking soldiers fired flame throwers to burn out enemy gun positions and pill boxes. Incendiary BOMBS containing magnesium, oil, jellied gasoline, or thermite were dropped by airplanes. These bombs scattered hot flames over a wide area. Phosphorus bombs were very destructive, as were the thermite bombs, which burned through steel.

Soldiers in the United States are trained in the use of protective clothing, first-aid, and gas masks. The Chemical Corps has special instruments to detect gas. The Lopair device detects small drops of liquid gas as far as a quarter of a mile away. The *aerosoloscope* counts minute particles of gas in the air.   P. F. D.

Chemistry (KEM-iss-tree) Chemistry is the science that deals with what the earth and the universe are made of. Except for empty space, the material of the universe is called *matter*. Chemistry is the science of what matter contains and how matter changes. The chemist experiments with matter to improve our understanding. The chemist's efforts have sometimes changed the course of history. The manufacturer, the doctor, and even the astronomer depend upon his work. To understand all matter and its changes is the object of chemistry.

Chemistry was used by man even before the year 1 A.D. Its roots lie in two basic interests—man's natural curiosity about his surroundings, and his early attempts to make things such as salt and vegetable dyes. Because man in early times did not use scientific methods, little progress was made toward making chemistry a science for about two thousand years.

Modern chemistry, as a science, truly began during the latter half of the 18th century. Three important ideas set off this new view from the first crude beginnings. There are: (1) the belief in fixed, characteristic properties of matter; (2) a need to relate the behavior of matter to its basic makeup; (3) increasing attention to the "how much" approach to chemical study, through MEASUREMENT and MATHEMATICS.

Today chemistry has become more and more mixed with physics, which also deals directly with the structure and behavior of matter. Physicists are more interested in energy, while chemists concentrate upon the structure and changes of matter.

THE ELEMENTS
(Arranged in order of atomic number and with atomic weights based on carbon-12 = 12.0000)

ATOMIC NUMBER	ELEMENT	SYMBOL	ATOMIC WEIGHT	ATOMIC NUMBER	ELEMENT	SYMBOL	ATOMIC WEIGHT	ATOMIC NUMBER	ELEMENT	SYMBOL	ATOMIC WEIGHT	ATOMIC NUMBER	ELEMENT	SYMBOL	ATOMIC WEIGHT
1	Hydrogen	H	1.0079	28	Nickel	Ni	58.70	55	Cesium	Cs	132.9054	82	Lead	Pb	207.2
2	Helium	He	4.00260	29	Copper	Cu	63.546	56	Barium	Ba	137.33	83	Bismuth	Bi	208.9804
3	Lithium	Li	6.941	30	Zinc	Zn	65.38	57	Lanthanum	La	138.9055	84	Polonium	Po	(209)
4	Beryllium	Be	9.01218	31	Gallium	Ga	69.72	58	Cerium	Ce	140.12	85	Astatine	At	(210)
5	Boron	B	10.81	32	Germanium	Ge	72.59	59	Praseodymium	Pr	140.9077	86	Radon	Rn	(222)
6	Carbon	C	12.011	33	Arsenic	As	74.9216	60	Neodymium	Nd	144.24	87	Francium	Fr	(223)
7	Nitrogen	N	14.0067	34	Selenium	Se	78.96	61	Promethium	Pm	(147)	88	Radium	Ra	226.0254
8	Oxygen	O	15.9994	35	Bromine	Br	79.904	62	Samarium	Sm	150.4	89	Actinium	Ac	(227)
9	Fluorine	F	18.998403	36	Krypton	Kr	83.80	63	Europium	Eu	151.96	90	Thorium	Th	232.0381
10	Neon	Ne	20.179	37	Rubidium	Rb	85.4678	64	Gadolinium	Gd	157.25	91	Protoactinium	Pa	231.0359
11	Sodium	Na	22.98977	38	Strontium	Sr	87.62	65	Terbium	Tb	158.9254	92	Uranium	U	238.029
12	Magnesium	Mg	24.305	39	Yttrium	Y	88.9059	66	Dysprosium	Dy	162.50	93	Neptunium	Np	237.0482
13	Aluminum	Al	26.98154	40	Zirconium	Zr	91.22	67	Holmium	Ho	164.9304	94	Plutonium	Pu	(244)
14	Silicon	Si	28.0855	41	Niobium	Nb	92.9064	68	Erbium	Er	167.26	95	Americium	Am	(243)
15	Phosphorus	P	30.97376	42	Molybdenum	Mo	95.94	69	Thulium	Tm	168.9342	96	Curium	Cm	(247)
16	Sulfur	S	32.06	43	Technetium	Tc	(97)	70	Ytterbium	Yb	173.04	97	Berkelium	Bk	(247)
17	Chlorine	Cl	35.453	44	Ruthenium	Ru	101.07	71	Lutecium	Lu	174.97	98	Californium	Cf	(251)
18	Argon	Ar	39.948	45	Rhodium	Rh	102.9055	72	Hafnium	Hf	178.49	99	Einsteinium	Es	(254)
19	Potassium	K	39.0983	46	Palladium	Pd	106.4	73	Tantalum	Ta	180.9479	100	Fermium	Fm	(257)
20	Calcium	Ca	40.08	47	Silver	Ag	107.868	74	Tungsten	W	183.85	101	Mendelevium	Md	(258)
21	Scandium	Sc	44.9559	48	Cadmium	Cd	112.41	75	Rhenium	Re	186.207	102	Nobelium	No	(259)
22	Titanium	Ti	47.90	49	Indium	In	114.82	76	Osmium	Os	190.2	103	Lawrencium	Lr	(260)
23	Vanadium	V	50.9414	50	Tin	Sn	118.69	77	Iridium	Ir	192.22	104	Kurchatovium	Ku	(257)
24	Chromium	Cr	51.996	51	Antimony	Sb	121.75	78	Platinum	Pt	195.09	105	Hahnium	Ha	(260)
25	Manganese	Mn	54.9380	52	Tellurium	Te	127.60	79	Gold	Au	196.9665	106	(not named)		
26	Iron	Fe	55.847	53	Iodine	I	126.9045	80	Mercury	Hg	200.59				
27	Cobalt	Co	58.9332	54	Xenon	Xe	131.30	81	Thallium	Tl	204.37				

Perhaps the most fundamental idea in chemistry is that of the *pure substance*. This is a sample of matter which has the same properties throughout; that is, each part behaves the same as every other part. Pure substances may exist in two forms, as an ELEMENT or a COMPOUND

An *element* is one form of the simplest possible kind of matter that can exist as such. The smallest possible particle of an element is an ATOM. For chemical purposes all atoms of any one element may be considered to be alike, although physically different kinds of atoms of the same element may exist. These different physical forms of the same element's atoms are called ISOTOPES, and the difference is one of weight. There are 106 recognized chemical elements, and all the world is made from these basic building blocks. Of these 106 different kinds of atoms, perhaps 50 are considered important from the standpoint of availability.

Chemists are accustomed to classifying the elements in terms of their positions upon a form of atomic chart called a *periodic table*. First prepared by the Russian chemist, DMITRI IVANOVITCH MENDELEEV, in 1869, and modified many times since then, the periodic table is to the chemist what a world globe is to a geographer. Each element is given a characteristic identifying number,

its *atomic number*. Hydrogen, the simplest element, has the number one, and so on through element number 106, which is the most complex.

All atoms are made up of three significant kinds of fundamental particles: *protons, neutrons,* and *electrons*. The protons and the neutrons are bound together in a tight little bundle called a *nucleus*. The electrons, very light particles, carry a negative electrical charge. In the normal atom, there is one ELECTRON circling outside for each PROTON within the nucleus; thus the total positive and negative electric charges balance each other. The normal atom is electrically neutral. When it gains or loses an electron, it becomes an ion.

Chemists once believed that the electrons orbited about the nucleus of the atom similar to the way that various planets in the solar system orbit about the sun, and indeed, many writers described the atom that way. But the latest research requires more careful description. Although the electrons do surround the neucleus, they cannot be thought of as particles in distinct orbits but must be pictured as rather indistinct clouds of negative electrical charges. The electrons surround the nucleus; each has a unit negative electrical charge. The number of electrons always equals the number of protons within the nucleus of that atom.

The atomic number of a given element is the number of protons within the nucleus of that kind of atom. Isotopes of the same element contain the same number of electrons and protons but differ in the number of neutrons contained in the nucleus. The neutrons are neutral and carry no electrical charge. They do not affect chemical properties of the atom.

The nucleus of an atom is indestructible by any chemical process. It may be split, of course, but by methods which are not chemical in approach. These are classified under NUCLEAR SCIENCE. The chemist concerns himself entirely with the electrons whose interactions, in a very real sense, hold the world together.

The electrons in an atom have been found to arrange themselves in definite patterns about the nucleus, some close, others relatively far away from it. In the larger atoms the innermost electrons remain practically untouchable, but the outermost electrons are often freely exchanged with those of other nearby atoms.

CHEMICAL REACTIONS

The ability of atoms to exchange electrons provides the basis for the most important classification of the elements into *metals* and *nonmetals*. Those elements which tend to *lose* electrons to other atoms are called *metals,* those that tend to *gain* electrons are *nonmetals*. The metals are most commonly found on the left side and the nonmetals on the right side of the periodic table, although exceptions do exist.

The most important practical fact in the behavior of atoms is that atoms may join together (or, as the chemist says, "react") to form even larger structures. They do this by gaining, losing, or sharing electrons. When two atoms thus combine, they are said to be held together by a *chemical bond.* A chemical bond is formed whenever the rearrangement of the electrons is a more stable system than are the arrangements of the original unbound atoms. A *chemical reaction* is the forming or breaking of chemical bonds to produce new substances. All chemical reactions occur because the stability of matter is increased thereby.

When several atoms thus bond together by sharing electrons, neither atom completely losing or gaining them, the resulting structure is called a MOLECULE, and the substance formed by billions of these is a *molecular compound*. On the other hand, an atom may lose or gain one or more electrons completely, forming a particle called an ION. The metallic elements lose electrons to form positive ions; the nonmetals gain them to form negative ions. The ions of opposite charge then may group together in regular, three-dimensional patterns called CRYSTALS. Ordinary table salt is a familiar example of such an *ionic crystalline compound.*

Due to the attraction which always exists between them, molecules, though electrically-neutral, may also group together to form molecular crystals. Table sugar and naphthalene (the latter used in moth crystals) are examples of *molecular crystal compounds.*

A constitutional chemical formula shows not only what atoms are present, but also how many atoms of each are present in each formula unit, as shown by the small numbers. For complex carbon compounds the chemist also makes use of *structural* formulas which, in addition, show the relative positions of the various atoms within the molecule.

Chemists combine formulas into chemical *equations,* a shorthand technique used to

SOME IMPORTANT METALS (ATOMS TEND TO LOSE ELECTRONS)	SOME IMPORTANT NON-METALS (ATOMS TEND TO GAIN ELECTRONS)
Sodium, Na	Fluorine, F
Potassium, K	Chlorine, Cl
Magnesium, Mg	Oxygen, O
Calcium, Ca	Bromine, Br
Zinc, Zn	Iodine, I
Aluminum, Al	Sulfur, S
Iron, Fe	Carbon, C
Lead, Pb	Nitrogen, N
Copper, Cu	Hydrogen, H
Tin, Sn	Silicon, Si
Silver, Ag	Phosphorus, P
Gold, Au	

SOME IMPORTANT CHEMICAL COMPOUNDS
BY CLASS OF COMPOUND

ACIDS:

Sulfuric acid, H_2SO_4
Hydrochloric acid, HCl
Nitric acid, HNO_3
Phosphoric acid, H_3PO_4
Carbonic acid, H_2CO_3
Acetic acid, $H(C_2H_3O_2)$

BASES:

Sodium hydroxide, NaOH
Potassium hydroxide, KOH
Calcium hydroxide, $Ca(OH)_2$
Magnesium hydroxide,
  $Mg(OH)_2$

SALTS:

Sodium chloride, NaCl
Sodium sulfate, Na_2SO_4
Potassium nitrate, KNO_3
Sodium hydrogen carbonate,
  $NaHCO_3$
Magnesium sulfate, $MgSO_4$
Calcium phosphate, $Ca_3(PO_4)_2$
Copper sulfate, $CuSO_4$

OXIDES:

Water, H_2O
Carbon dioxide, CO_2
Sulfur dioxide, SO_2
Calcium oxide, CaO
Aluminum oxide, Al_2O_3
Iron oxide, Fe_2O_3

CARBON CHAIN, ORGANIC, COMPOUNDS:

Ethyl alcohol, C_2H_5OH
Table sugar, Sucrose, $C_{12}H_{22}O_{11}$
Grape sugar, Glucose, $C_6H_{12}O_6$
Natural gas, Methane, CH_4
Carbon tetrachloride, CCl_4
Ethyl ether, $(C_2H_5)_2O$

Soap, $C_{17}H_{35}COONa$
Acetone $(CH_3)_2CO$
Glycerine, $C_3H_5(OH)_3$
Benzene, C_6H_6
Acetylene, C_2H_2
Formaldehyde, H_2CO

STRUCTURAL FORMULA FOR ACETYL-SALICYLIC ACID, SODIUM SALT (COMMONLY CALLED ASPIRIN)

H = Hydrogen
C = Carbon
O = Oxygen

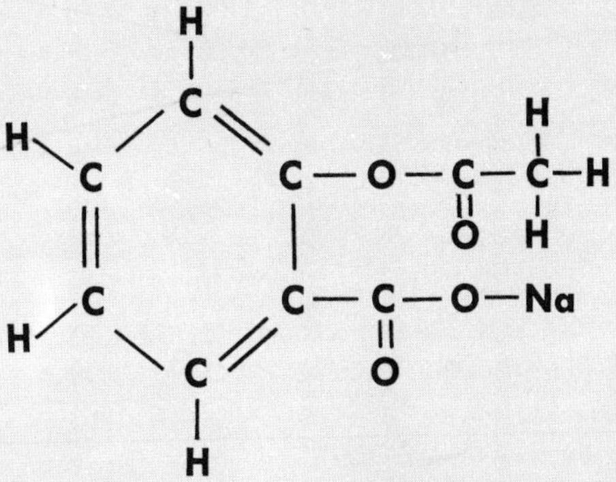

Each line between atoms represents one shared electron pair (one chemical bond)

Note that the structural formula shows the relative position of each atom in the molecule

study the course of a chemical reaction. The chemical equation representing the reaction between sulfuric acid and sodium hydroxide is shown below:

$$H_2SO_4 + 2NaOH \rightarrow 2H_2O + Na_2SO_4$$

sulfuric acid + sodium hydroxide yields water + sodium sulfate

A correct chemical equation must be balanced. This means the total number of atoms on both sides must be equal. Furthermore, not all equations which may be written actually represent true chemical reactions. Only by experiment is it possible to determine which reactions will occur.

BASIC OPERATIONS OF CHEMISTRY

The chemist's workplace is called a LABORATORY. Here he performs those experiments upon which true scientific knowledge must depend. Modern chemistry has become so complex that it is quite impossible to describe in detail all of a chemist's laboratory work. However there are four classical operations frequently performed in chemical laboratory work. (1) *Solution:* A solid or a liquid is intimately mixed with another liquid so that the molecules or ions of the two substances actually diffuse among each other. (2) *Crystallization:* The desired compound, previously dissolved, is caused to leave the solution and settle on the bottom of the vessel in the form of pure crystals, while the undesired substances (impurities) remain dissolved. (3) *Distillation:* A liquid is carefully heated to convert it into a vapor. The vapor is then passed through a cooled tube and recondensed into a liquid. In this manner substances boiling at different temperatures may be separated. (4) *Quantitative combustion:* A weighed sample of the substance to be examined is burned in an atmosphere of pure oxygen, and the gaseous products formed are absorbed and weighed. Spectrography, ion-exchange, and electrolytic deposition are some other methods widely used by chemists today.

American Oil Co.

A modern chemistry laboratory

BRANCHES OF CHEMISTRY

Because literally the whole world of matter is subject to chemical study, each chemist has found it necessary to concentrate his attention on one of the many specialized fields of this subject. Some of these specialized *fields* are: (1) *General or Inorganic Chemistry,* which investigates principles and methods applicable to many other fields. (2) *Physical Chemistry* is the theoretical and mathematical study of the chemical reaction itself. Here the chemist and physicist work so closely together that it is often impossible to distinguish their work. (3) *Analytical Chemistry* is the study and practice of methods for determining just what substances are present within a specific quantity of matter, and exactly how much of each is present. (4) *Organic Chemistry* is the study of the carbon chain compounds. (5) BIOCHEMISTRY deals with the compounds and reactions in living organisms. (6) *Pharmaceutical chemistry* is the chemical study of drugs and medicines. (7) *Industrial Chemistry* and *Chemical Engineering* apply chemical principles to the satisfaction of man's material need and comfort. (8) *Geochemistry* considers the chemical aspects of the earth's structure. (9) *Chemical Education* is becoming increasingly important every day. It concerns itself with the teaching of chemistry.   C. F. R.

SEE ALSO: BOHR THEORY, COMPOUND, ELEMENTS, ION, ORGANIC COMPOUNDS, RUTHERFORD THEORY

Chemotherapy (KEE-mow-THAIR-a-pee) Chemotherapy is the use of DRUGS to kill organisms that produce disease. It usually refers to the treatment of CANCER with drugs.

Most living CELLS are somewhat poisoned by chemotherapy. As otherwise healthy cells are damaged, patients often develop side effects, including hair loss, nausea, stomach pain, and increased risk of infection. Chemo-

therapy is based on the fact that cancer cells grow quickly and may be killed before normal cells are destroyed. Benefits may be temporary, rarely lasting more than two years for some LEUKEMIA victims.   J.H.

SEE ALSO: MEDICINE

Cherry It is a shrub or tree with simple leaves. The flowers are perfect and usually white. The fruit is one of the most important foods of birds and mammals.

The sour cherry tree is about 25 feet (7.62 meters) tall, has white flowers, 3-inch (7.62 centimeter) leaves, and a red tart fruit. The sweet cherry is about 40 feet (12.19 meters) high, has leaves up to 6 inches (15.24 centimeters) long, white flowers, and yellow or red drupes. The choke cherry is a shrub or small tree with purplish fruit. The black cherry is valuable timber. The prussic acid in the leaves, seeds, and bark is harmful if eaten by animals. All plants belong to the family Rosaceae. Ground cherry is a wild vine of the nightshade family.   H.J.C.

Chert see Rocks

Chestnut see Nuts

Chickadee The chickadee is a small gray bird with a black cap, black bib, and white cheeks. It has a long tail and a short stubby bill. The active chickadee is smaller than a SPARROW. It can hang upside down when searching for insects.

The bird's name comes from its clear distinct call — *chick-a-dee-dee-dee.* The chickadee does not migrate. It feeds on insects as well as berries and seeds. The chickadee lays from 6 to 10 eggs. The eggs are white with reddish-brown speckles.   W.J.K.

Chickadee
Mrs. Allan D. Cruickshank

Helen J. Challand

The many varieties of domestic chickens (right) probably came from the wild jungle fowl (left)

Chicken A chicken is a tame bird commonly seen on farms. Its flesh and its eggs are used for food. The chicken was first domesticated, or tamed, over 3000 years ago. There are now more than 100 varieties, or kinds, of chickens. They are all believed to have come from a wild *jungle fowl* of southwest Asia.

Modern varieties produce better meat and larger eggs than wild chickens. They have been developed by many years of careful, selective breeding. The Plymouth Rocks, Rhode Island Reds, Leghorns, and New Hampshires are common American varieties. Another variety is the little bantam.

Capons are also raised on poultry farms. A *capon* is a rooster (male) that has had its sex glands (testes) removed. This is called *castration,* and is done when the chicks are 8-10 weeks old. Capons develop hen-like combs and wattles. They are easier to fatten, grow larger, and have more tender meat than normal roosters.   J. C. K.
SEE ALSO: FOWL

Chicken pox Chicken pox is a disease of children, although adults can contract it if they have not had it in their childhood. It is very contagious, or catching. It is not related to SMALLPOX although when people were naming this disease—about 1530 A.D.—they thought it was little smallpox. The medical name for the condition is *varicella.*

The infection is caused by a VIRUS. Often the first sign of chicken pox is the appearance of small blisters on the chest and back, with a fever, upset stomach, and headache. Sometimes the eruption appears on the face and spreads over the body. The blisters will appear in clusters at 12- to 24-hour intervals and soon turn to scabs. Thus, in chicken pox, a person has blisters and scabs appearing at the same time. This is in contrast to the far more deadly disease smallpox, where all the blisters appear at one time, followed by scabs and deep scars.

Chicken pox spreads by infected droplets sneezed or coughed by persons coming down with the disease, before the blisters appear. When a person is exposed to chicken pox, about two weeks will elapse before the disease erupts.   B. M. H.

Chicle Chicle is used in making chewing gum. It comes from the gum of the tropical, evergreen, *Sapodilla* tree. The Mayan Indians chewed chicle long before America was discovered. The Sapodilla tree grows mainly in Florida, Mexico, and Central America.

The bark of the Sapodilla tree contains a milky substance that is chicle. When the bark is slashed, the chicle oozes out. The chicle is then gathered and boiled down to get rid of most of the water. Then it is formed into blocks and sent to chewing gum factories. Today, about nine-tenths of all chewing gum is produced in the United States.   M. R. L.

Chicory (CHICK-uh-ree) Roadsides in early autumn are often dotted with wild chicory. It is a hardy plant which grows year after year. The tall, slender stem has a white juice. The taproot is fleshy. The usually blue flowers appear all summer.

Chicory

The chicory plants belong in the composite family, so the "flower" is actually made up of many showy ray flowers. One variety, commonly a weed in the United States, develops a rootstock which, when roasted, is often used instead of coffee. A second variety, grown mainly in Europe, is also called *French endive* or *Witloof chicory*. The young stems and greens are used as a salad vegetable after boiling the plant parts to get rid of the biting taste. The young root is a vegetable, cooked as carrots would be.   H. J. C.

Chigger see Mite

Chimpanzee (tchimm-pan-ZEE) The chimpanzee is an anthropoid APE. Anthropoid means "like man." Its face has an almost human appearance. Four long fingers and a thumb on each hand make grasping and handling objects easy. Chimpanzees also have "thumbs" instead of big toes on their feet. They have no tails. Chimpanzees sometimes grow as tall as 5 feet (1.52 meters) and have been known to weigh 160 pounds (72.57 kilograms).

Chimpanzees have been found in Africa from the jungles of French Guinea to Western Uganda and the dark thick jungles of the Congo. They do not like the plains and the open country.

Chimpanzees are *arboreal,* which means "tree-dwellers." Throughout the jungles and forests they travel swinging from limb to limb. As they travel they make a wide

Chimpanzee
Courtesy Society For Visual Education, Inc.

variety of sounds. The most common one is a loud, high-pitched cry. For sleeping, chimpanzees build nests high up in trees. The female gives birth to one baby at a time.

The chimpanzee's diet may consist of fruits, buds, bananas, small animals, birds' eggs and insects. Their preference, though, seems to be more for plants rather than animals or animal products.

In captivity the young are very friendly and sociable but as they grow older they become more withdrawn and unsociable, even dangerous. They can and often do develop human-like attachments to man. Chimpanzees live from 20 to 24 years and are of special interest to scientists because of their striking similarity to man. They are curious, imitative and appear to have a keener problem-solving ability than any other animal known to man. Mechanical skills can be developed in them and their sense of rhythm is very strong. In tests of intelligence they have been known to compare favorably with three-year-old children. They can be taught to master such tasks as eating with a spoon, a knife and a fork. Because of their great similarities to man it is possible that they might serve well as substitutes for man in scientific experimentation and research.   G. A. D.

Chinch bug see Bugs

Chinchilla The chinchilla is a small rodent found in the mountains of South America. It is about 10 inches (25.4 centimeters) long and has large ears, a bushy tail and silver-gray fur.

The chinchilla is very shy and timid. It hastily hides when disturbed. It feeds on plants, fruits, grains, and roots. It uses its front paws to hold the food.

The wild chinchilla is becoming extinct. It has been killed for its valuable fur. Today chinchillas are raised commercially.   W.J.K.
SEE ALSO: RODENTIA

Chinook Wind A chinook is a very warm, dry irregular wind that occurs in many mountainous areas. Because it is extremely dry and warm, it can evaporate as much as 26 centimeters (10.24 inches) of snow in a day.

Courtesy Society For Visual Education, Inc.
Chipmunk

Chipmunk Chipmunks are in the squirrel family. They are also called striped ground squirrels. Chipmunks feed on seeds, nuts, and fruit. The coats of both sexes are alike. Their backs have a rusty brown shading, with grayish brown on the sides and cheeks. On the back are stripes.

The number of stripes and their brightness depends upon the species. Chipmunks live all over the United States and Canada. Eastern and western chipmunks are now put in different groups (genera). Eastern ones are larger, have more and broader stripes, and have brighter coats than the western species.

Chipmunks burrow without marking their burrows with piles of soil like the woodchucks. Soil is carted away, probably in their cheek pouches. Burrows have several entrances and a nesting chamber. In the spring, three to five young are born. Often there are two litters a year. Chipmunks hibernate in the winter. They may wake up during that time to eat stored food.   J. C. K.

SEE ALSO: RODENTIA

Chitin (KI-tin) Chitin is the horny substance found in the shells of CRABS, outer coverings of insects, and hard parts of similar creatures and some plants. Pure chitin is a white powder which is very difficult to dissolve.

Chitin is a long chain of modified sugar molecules. The basic glucose molecule (sugar) has two new organic groups. These replace one hydroxyl (OH) group in glucose. One is an amino group (NH_2). Amino groups occur in all proteins. The other is an acetyl group ($COCH_3$). It is derived from acetic acid, commonly called vinegar.

There are a number of chemically treated chitin products now being used in many industries. Recently the drug, cosmetic and textile industries have been using modified chitin products as thickeners and protective coatings.

A general formula for chitin is $C_{30}H_{50}N_4O_{19}$, for which the molecular weight is 770.73.   M. S.

SEE ALSO: CARBOHYDRATES, INSECTA

Chiton (KYE-tuhn) A chiton is a small mollusk that has eight valves to its shell, one foot, and no eyes. The valves are the sections of its shell. They overlap one another as do the shingles on a house. Underneath the shell the animal's body is very soft. Most of the body is a large powerful foot which helps the chiton move.

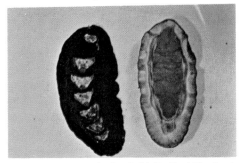

Courtesy Society For Visual Education, Inc.
Chiton is found in rock pools at the seashore.

This primitive mollusk has the basic characteristics of the more advanced members of its group. It has a complete digestive system, kidneys, a three-chambered heart, and a ladder-like nervous system. Its insignificant head is merely the narrow forward end of the foot and possesses a mouth but no eyes. The shell of eight calcareous plates is secreted by the mantle. Its diet consists mainly of algae.   H. J. C.

SEE ALSO: MOLLUSCA

Chloride (KLO-ride) A chloride is a compound made by CHLORINE in combination with certain other elements.

The chlorides, especially the common ones like sodium chloride—common table salt—are a useful family of compounds.

The chlorides are derivatives of HYDRO-CHLORIC ACID. Each chlorine atom in a chloride is in a −1 oxidation state which means it is actually an ION with a negative charge of 1. The test for the presence of the chloride ion in solution is to add silver nitrate. If a white precipitate forms which cannot be dissolved by nitric acid and can be dissolved in ammonium hydroxide, the chloride ion is present.

Sodium chloride is the most important of metallic chloride salts. It is the starting point from which man gets all his SODIUM and chlorine as well as the source of many useful chemicals, among them hydrochloric acid. It is used in food preservation, leather tanning and many other processes.

Other important chlorides are calcium chloride, used to melt ice on roads; titanium tetrachloride which provides smoke for sky-writing; silver chloride, for photographic development; and aluminum chloride, a catalyst in the petroleum and dye-making industries.   E. R. B.

SEE ALSO: COMPOUND

Chlorination see Chlorine, Water

Chlorine (KLO-reen) Chlorine (C1) is an element which usually occurs as a greenish-yellow gas, two and one-half times as heavy as air. It belongs, along with bromine, iodine, fluorine, and astatine, to a family group of ELE-MENTS called the *halogens*. It has an irritating odor and is poisonous in large quantities. It is useful, however, as a bleach and a germ-killer. Chlorine is never found free in nature but is found combined with other elements, as chloride salts and other compounds.

Chlorine was discovered by the Swedish chemist K. W. Scheele in 1774. He thought he had made an OXIDE, and it wasn't until 1810 that SIR HUMPHRY DAVY proved that it was a new element.

Chlorine is manufactured industrially by ELECTROLYSIS of either a solution of sodium chloride or molten sodium chloride. The chlorine is collected at the positive pole of an electrolytic cell, piped off, and liquefied by compression. It is then shipped in steel tanks. Ocean water and inland salt deposits, which can be treated with water to form salt solutions or BRINE, are sources of chlorine.

Chlorine has the atomic number 17. Its atomic weight is 35.453. Because of the way the electrons are arranged in the chlorine atom, chlorine combines readily with other elements to form hundreds of inorganic and organic compounds.

Chlorine alone and in compounds is very important industrially. Over 500,000,000 pounds (227,000,000 kilograms) are used annually in the United States. Its greatest use is as a BLEACHING AGENT. It bleaches very rapidly by a reaction with water, in which oxygen is freed and combines with dyes in paper and cloth to form colorless compounds. This bleaching action can be observed at home by using a weak solution of ink and water and a teaspoonful of liquid laundry bleach as the source of chlorine.

Chlorine is also a powerful germ killer. By oxidation it kills bacteria which cause typhoid and many other diseases. Chlorine is used extensively in treating drinking water (1 drop liquid chlorine in 50 gals. (189 l.) water kills all bacteria), swimming pools, and sewage.

Another important use of chlorine is in the manufacture of other chemicals, principally HYDROCHLORIC ACID. Some of the other chemical products are CARBON TETRA-CHLORIDE, CHLOROFORM, freon gas (used in refrigerators), and coal tar dyes. It is also used in extracting metals from their ores and in purifying oil.   E. R. B.

Chloroform (KLO-ruh-form) Chloroform is a chemical substance composed of carbon, hydrogen and chlorine. It is a clear, colorless liquid with a sweet, burning taste and a sharp, sweetish smell. One of its best known uses was as one of the first general ANESTHET-ICS for surgery. It is used widely as a chemical solvent and in some medicines.

Three scientists shared in the discovery of chloroform about 1831—Eugene Soubeiran of France, Justus von Leibig of Germany, and Samuel Guthrie of the United States, who called it *chloric ether*. It was first used as an anesthetic in 1847 by Sir James Simpson, a Scottish physician.

Chloroform's chemical formula is $CHCl_3$. It is often made from ethyl alcohol. It is not often used today because it may damage the metabolic processes of some organs in the body, such as the liver.   G.A.D.

SEE ALSO: PHARMACOLOGY

Chloromycetin see Antibiotics

WHY IS CHLOROPHYLL NECESSARY IN PLANTS THAT MAKE FOOD?

Materials: Plant, alcohol, containers, iodine, aluminum foil

1 Put a green leaf in a small glass of alcohol. Set this in a larger container of boiling water. Never boil alcohol directly over a flame.
2 After several minutes the alcohol will become green and the leaf white.
3 Test for starch by applying a few drops of iodine to the leaf. It will turn a dark blue if starch is present.
4 Cover one entire leaf on a plant with foil. Permit it to grow for three days.
5 Remove the foil. The leaf has lost some of its green coloring. Test for starch.

Chlorophyll (KLOR-uh-fill) Chlorophyll is the green material in plants. Plants are not able to make food without it. Since animals lack chlorophyll, they depend on green plants for food.

Chlorophyll, using the energy from light, can change CARBON DIOXIDE and water into sugar and release oxygen. This process is basic to all food production for living things. A chemical formula for chlorophyll is a combination of these two pigments—$C_{55}H_{72}O_5N_4Mg$ and $C_{55}H_{70}O_6N_4Mg$.

When sunlight or artificial light is not sufficient, the chlorophyll fades out in leaves and permits other colors to show through. This occurs in the fall and gives trees in autumn their beautiful colors. As the sun's rays become less direct, the chlorophyll gradually weakens to reveal red, yellow, and brown pigments.

Chlorophyll occurs in bodies called *chlor-*oplasts*. These are oval, and surrounded by a double membrane. Inside, membranes form stacks of disks or *grana*. Grana are interconnected by paired membranes (*lamellae*). Chlorophyll and other pigments are arranged on the grana.   J. C. K.
SEE ALSO: CARBON CYCLE, PHOTOSYNTHESIS

Chocolate see Cocoa

Cholera (KAHL-uh-ruh) Cholera is a deadly infectious disease caused by a comma-shaped bacterium which infects intestines. There have been epidemics in the United States in the past, but sanitation, sewage disposal, and treatment of water supplies have rid this country of it.

It is called Asiatic cholera because epidemics still prevail in India, China, and other countries of the Far East. Cholera is passed from person to person mainly through contaminated water. An individual infected develops abdominal cramps, nausea, vomiting, and severe diarrhea. The continuous diarrhea results in loss of enormous amounts of water and life-sustaining chemicals from the body. The patient dies in six to eight hours if the chemicals are not replaced by treatment. This is one of the epidemic diseases which has altered the course of history. A vaccine is available for prevention.   B.M.H.

Cholesterol   (kuh-LESS-tuh-rahl) Cholesterol is a fat which is found in the human body and in other large animals. It does not look like other fats which one sees on meat in a butcher shop. Cholesterol in its pure form is a white material which looks like sugar or salt. It is made up of tiny CRYSTALS which can be seen under the microscope.

The cholesterol of the body is found in fatty tissues, but especially in the brain, spinal cord, and nerve tissue. It is also found in fatty foods such as egg yolk, dairy products, solid shortenings, and cooking fats made from animal fat. Corn oil and peanut oil are also fats, but they come from vegetables and do not contain cholesterol.

For laboratory and other uses pure cholesterol is obtained from the spinal cord of cattle. It is also found in large amounts in wool grease or LANOLIN. It is probably the cholesterol content more than anything else which has made lanolin so popular in beauty and healing creams. Also, cholesterol-containing lotions are reported to have a soothing effect on irritated skin.

In addition to the normal places where cholesterol is found in the body, it is also found in gallstones and sometimes too much of it is found in the blood. Scientists are still trying to find out whether or not too much cholesterol in the blood can cause hardening of the arteries and heart disease. However, there is proof that using peanut or corn oil instead of butter for cooking will lower the amount of cholesterol found in the blood.

The chemical formula for pure cholesterol is $C_{27}H_{46}O$. The molecular weight is 386.64. Vitamin D and certain HORMONES of the body have chemical formulas similar to cholesterol.   M. S.

Chordata (kohr-DAY-tuh) A cloth tent will fall down unless it is held up with stiff poles. In the same way, the soft bodies of people are held up with strong inner skeletons. People belong to a large group of animals called *Chordates* which means, "with a cord."

At some time during their lives, all chordates have a *notochord* or "back cord." This is a stiff, elastic rod which runs along the back. It allows the animal to bend from side to side and keeps the body from folding like an accordian.

As a child grows taller, he needs stronger bones to hold a larger body.

Many of the large chordates develop a stronger backbone made of small bones, called *vertebrae*. Just as a coiled rod bends more easily than a straight rod, the vertebrae allow the animal to bend and twist more easily. Mammals, birds, fish, reptiles, and amphibians are chordates with backbones made of vertebrae. They are known as *vertebrates*.

But some chordates are small and poorly developed. If a person walks along the ocean beach at low tide, he will find the lower chordates. He may be squirted by the small *tunicate,* which attaches itself to a rock and draws food through a funnel. He will have to dig in the wet sand to find the *acorn worm* and *amphioxus.* In these animals, the notochord is the only skeleton. Some of them lose the notochord as they become adults. These animals are often called *invertebrate* chordates or chordates "without vertebrae."

Although the chordates make up in numbers of species less than 1% of the animal kingdom, this phylum is one of the most interesting. It contains man and many of the animals important to man. Some of the most advanced animals are found among the chordates. Since they have explored every type of environment, they are found on land, in sand and mud, on rocks, in fresh and salt water and in the air. Many have powerful muscles and paired appendages, so that they can travel great distances at high speed. With strong supporting skeletons, some grow to tremendous size. The blue whale, for example, reaches a length of over 100 feet (30.48 meters).

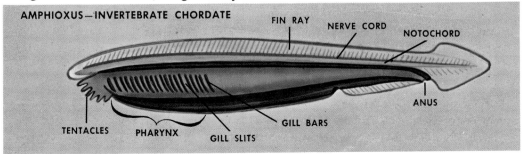

AMPHIOXUS—INVERTEBRATE CHORDATE

FIN RAY NERVE CORD NOTOCHORD

ANUS

TENTACLES PHARYNX GILL SLITS GILL BARS

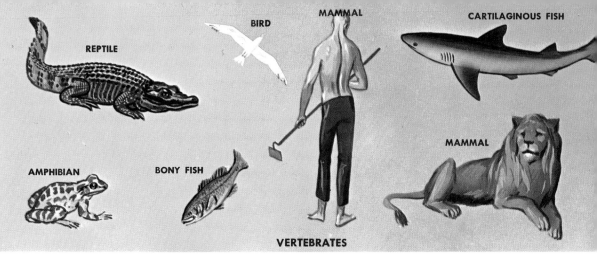

REPTILE · BIRD · MAMMAL · CARTILAGINOUS FISH · AMPHIBIAN · BONY FISH · MAMMAL

VERTEBRATES

The chordates are also distinguished by having a long, hollow, nerve cord, which extends the length of the back. Among some of the vertebrates with a distinct head, the nerve cord is enlarged to form a BRAIN.

At some time during their development, all chordates have *gill slits*. These open through the sides of the pharynx, or cavity between the mouth and the opening to the digestive tract. A continuous channel extends from the mouth to the pharynx to the exterior. Among aquatic animals, like the lower chordates, lamprey eel, and fish, the gill slits are used for breathing throughout adult life. However, in air-breathing animals, the gills appear only in the embryo. As the animal develops, LUNGS pouch out from the pharynx and replace the gills as a means of breathing. Lungs and gills appear at the same time in salamanders and lungfish.

CHORDATES WITHOUT SKULLS

Although there are many classes of chordates, there are really two main divisions. The *acraniates* are without a cranium or skull, since they have no head. They also lack vertebrae and appendages for locomotion. Included in this group are the primitive marine chordates, the acorn worms, tunicates and amphioxi. As adults, they closely resemble the invertebrates.

The tiny marine acorn worm looks very much like an earthworm. Behind a long snout or proboscis, which is used for burrowing in the sand, there is a short thick collar, followed by a long trunk. The mouth is located on the bottom surface, at the point where the collar and snout are joined. Extending from the collar into the snout is the short, poorly-developed notochord, which supports the proboscis.

Common on ship bottoms, wharves, and other firm surfaces are the tunicates with their sac-like bodies. These animals surround themselves with a covering or tunic of cellulose, a substance common to the plant kingdom. The free-swimming LARVA, which looks like a tadpole has a well-developed notochord in the tail as well as a primitive brain. However, it cements itself to a hard surface and becomes transformed. The tail, nerve cord, brain, and notochord disappear. Through two siphons, raised on the sides of the body, foods enter and wastes are eliminated.

Another sand-burrower is the small, slender, fish-shaped amphioxus, or lancelet. The word *Amphioxus* really means, "pointed at both ends." Since it has a highly developed, segmented body, this animal closely relates to the vertebrates. For the first time, the muscles appear in tiny bundles, called *somites.* A notochord, which extends the length of the body, remains throughout life.

CHORDATES WITH SKULLS

The *Craniata,* or *Vertebrata,* make up the second main chordate division. Since these animals have a head, there is a cranium, or skull, which houses the brain. For locomotion, they have well-developed fins, limbs or wings. Although the notochord appears in the embryo, it is later surrounded by the vertebrae, in the adult animal. Among higher vertebrates, the notochord is replaced completely by the vertebrae.

The FISH or PISCES make up the large group of aquatic vertebrates. Included with the eel-shaped jawless fish are the hagfish and lampreys. For these animals, the head end forms a funnel-shaped sucker and the notochord forms the center of vertebrae.

The cartilaginous fish, like the SHARK, SKATE, and RAY, develop a vertebral column and a skeleton of cartilage. Nearly half of all vertebrate species are made up of the scaly-skinned bony fish which develop a strong skeleton, consisting mainly of bone.

Included among the four-legged vertebrates, or *tetrapods,* are the amphibians, reptiles, birds (Aves) and mammals. While a few like the sea turtle are aquatic, most tetrapods live on land. Although some, like the NEWT and SALAMANDER retain their gills as adults, even these animals breathe with lungs.

Chordates reach the highest level of development. With bilateral symmetry, a distinct head and tail region appear. With three body layers, chordates have well-developed organ systems. Reproduction is sexual and each individual has a pair of reproductive organs.   E. P. L.
SEE ALSO: AMPHIBIANS, BIRD, PISCES, REPTILIA, MAMMALIA

Choroid coat   see Eye

Chromatic   see Lens, man-made

Chromatophores   (KROH-mah-tuh-fohrz) Chromatophores are cells which, by changing shapes, cause variations in the skin color of certain fish, amphibians, and some invertebrates.
SEE: SQUID

Chromium Chromium is one of the elements. It is a very hard, crystalline metal, silvery in appearance. *Chromite* is the chief ore used to prepare chromium. Chromium is widely used to plate various automobile parts. Some gems, such as emerald and jade, owe their beautiful colors to small amounts of chromium present as an impurity.

Chromium was discovered by a French chemist, L.N. Vauquelin, in 1797, but for many years it had no special use. Now it is used in making special steel alloys of great hardness and tensile strength. Along with nickel, chromium is used in making stainless steel. Its atomic weight is 52.01 and its atomic number is 24. The melting point of chromium is 1890° C. (3434° F.). Objects to be plated with chromium are first plated with copper or nickel and polished to a hard shine because chromium is hard to buff. The shine of the metal underneath shows through. The United States must import chromite ore.   J.H.D

Chromosomes Chromosomes appear as solid, darkly stained bodies during the middle stages of cell division (mitosis). They come from a condensation of threadlike nuclear materials in cells not undergoing division. Chromosomes contain chemical areas for the control of inheritance. These areas are called GENES. Genes are no longer believed to be definite particles.

Chromosomes occur in pairs. The number of pairs in a given species is constant. For example, all the cells of corn have 20 chromosomes, all humans 46, all fruit flies 8. Genes are also paired. A pair of genes may affect the inheritance of a single characteristic but not always in the same way. A pair of genes may affect coat color. One of them may bring about white coats and the other black. Pairs of genes are called *alleles.*

Chromosomes are composed of nucleic acid and proteins called *histones.* Experiments have shown that histones are not active in inheritance, so their presence is usually ignored. Nucleic acids contain the genes.

Nucleic acids are formed of subunits called *nucleotides.* Four kinds of nucleotides join together in different arrangements to make the molecules of a chromosome. Nucleotides are made of phosphorus, a five-carbon sugar, and one of four organic bases.   J. C. K.

Chronometer   see Clocks

Chrysalis   see Metamorphosis

During the cleavage of a fertilized Ascaris egg, the chromosomes become clearly visible
Photo-micrograph by National Teaching Aids, Inc.

Web arrangement of 22 chromosomes in a bug and star pattern of 8 chromosomes in a parasitic hookworm

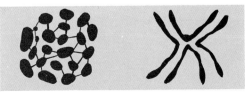

Chrysanthemum

Cineraria

Chrysanthemum (krih-SANTH-uh-mum) These flowering plants are called mums for short. They look like a single flower but are really many blooms on the top of one flower stalk. They produce the blossom and fruit in the autumn when the nights are long and the days are short.

There are three groups of mums. The large single variety has many *disk* flowers with a ring of *ray* flowers around the center. The large double type has a tiny cluster of disk flowers surrounded by many long ray flowers. The pompons possess a compact head of short blooms. The small mums in this group are called button chrysanthemums.

Mums range in height from 9 to 30 inches (22.86 to 76.2 centimeters). The flowers appear in every color except blue. The fruit is a dry, indehiscent achene. The leaves and flowers are highly scented with aromatic oils. Some mums are annuals but most are perennials. They belong to the Compositae family. H.J.C.

SEE ALSO: COMPOSITE FLOWER

Cicada see Bugs, Insecta

Cilia Cilia are hair-like processes of protoplasm which occur on the surfaces of some cells. Their vibrations direct the movements of particles in the body fluid or actually serve as a means of locomotion for the animal.

Cineraria (sin-uh-RARE-ee-uh) The cineraria is a flowering plant. It is usually grown indoors or in the greenhouse. This bushy plant grows from 1 to 2.5 feet (.3-.76 meters) tall. The leaves are very large and feel like velvet. The flowers look like small daisies. They may be blue, pink, purple, red, or white. M.R.L.

SEE ALSO: BLIGHT, MILDEW

Cinnabar (SIN-uh-bahr) Cinnabar is the only important ore from which MERCURY is obtained. Cinnabar is red sulfide of mercury. Its formula is HgS. A pigment called *vermillion* is made from this bright-red ore. Fine hard grades of cinnabar are carved and polished for use as gems.

Cinnamon (SIN-uh-mun) This is a small evergreen shrub or tree. Cinnamon is also the name for a spice, the middle layer of bark which is taken from this plant. The oil in the cells gives the flavor.

Circadian rhythm (ser-KAY-dee-an) Circadian rhythm is a behavior pattern based on approximately 24-hour cycles. It is an internal clock affected by light, darkness, temperature, or humidity. Both plants and animals can exhibit a circadian rhythm.

Cockroaches, bats, and moths are active at night. Fruit flies come out at dawn. Some aquatic organisms come and go with the tides. Certain plants display a sleep-movement rhythm at night and then raise their leaves in daylight.

Scientists have difficulty explaining the cause of circadian rhythms. Theories center around light, gravity, electromagnetic fields, or something in the body. H.J.C.

SEE ALSO: BIOLOGICAL CLOCK

Circle see Earth, Geometry

Circuits, see Electricity

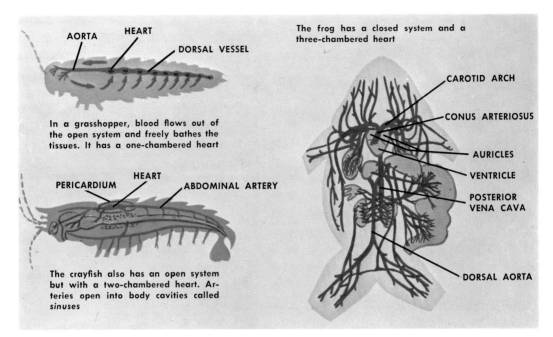

AORTA HEART
DORSAL VESSEL

In a grasshopper, blood flows out of the open system and freely bathes the tissues. It has a one-chambered heart

HEART
PERICARDIUM ABDOMINAL ARTERY

The crayfish also has an open system but with a two-chambered heart. Arteries open into body cavities called sinuses

The frog has a closed system and a three-chambered heart

CAROTID ARCH
CONUS ARTERIOSUS
AURICLES
VENTRICLE
POSTERIOR VENA CAVA
DORSAL AORTA

Circulatory system The circulatory system and its main organ, the heart, pump, feed, cool, warm, protect, and keep the body well. The HEART is the hardest working organ in the body. It has to squeeze and push, suck and pull steadily, without missing a beat throughout one's whole life.

Attached to every heart in animals from the grasshopper, worm, crayfish, reptile, fish, frog, bird, and finally to man is a system of outgoing and incoming pipes that are called *blood vessels*. These pipes carry food, air, chemicals, water, and enzymes throughout the body to keep it alive and well. The system even has an "army" of billions of white cells to protect it. If the circulatory system breaks or is torn open, it plugs itself automatically with tiny discs called *platelets*. These jam up at the opening to plug the break and are glued together by a substance in the blood called *fibrin*. This is how a scab forms after a cut.

The heart is an amazing engine. It is a pump, designed to keep the BLOOD moving. It starts working before the body is completely built and works continuously as long as one lives. Every seven seconds the heart pumps 2 gallons (7.57 liters) of blood over the circulatory system (a mile or 1½ kilometers long) for every second of every day, even during sleep.

The circulatory system was millions of years in developing. It is important to understand the parts of the body that make blood circulation possible.

First there are *arteries* that carry blood from the heart to the lungs and body. Arteries are present in all circulatory systems. In fact, the first pumping organ was an artery that throbbed.

Then there are *veins,* found only in the later animals. These carry the blood from the lungs and body back to the heart. They are smaller in size than the arteries.

Between these two kinds of "pipes" is a pump called the *heart*. Scientists think that the heart began as a tube that squeezed the blood from a source of concentration out through the whole body. Body organs in simpler forms were fed in much the same way as the land is flooded when a river overflows. The GRASSHOPPER has this type of

✳ THINGS TO DO

HOW DOES BLOOD CIRCULATE THROUGH THE HEART?

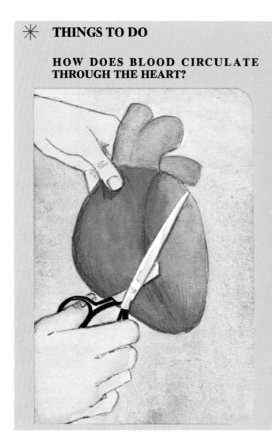

Materials: Very sharp scissors; razor blade; and a pencil or two; lamb, veal, or pork heart, FRESH

1 Find the thick side of the heart—this is the side that pumps to the body.
2 The large white vessels at the top are the branches of the aorta. Stick your finger down into one of these vessels, gently probing until you reach the chamber inside.
3 Cut with the scissors along the surface of the heart, using the finger as a runner for one point of the scissors. Do the same on the other side and you will have the heart opened up so that you can see for yourself what a marvel of efficiency and perfection it is. Look for the valves; these work steadily and perfectly for years. Can you think of a valve that man has made that is as good?
4 With a piece of string trace the flow of blood through the heart.   **L. M.**

circulatory system. In the grasshopper the blood is squeezed along in much the same manner as a swimmer squirting his friends by squeezing his hands in the water.

In the earthworm its blood system is a closed system with ten hearts or lobes (swellings) that do the squeezing (throbbing) and move the blood along. The hearts connect the dorsal and ventral blood vessels. The blood flows toward the anterior end in the dorsal vessel with valves preventing any back flow. Leaving the hearts, the blood is pumped out the ventral vessel in a posterior direction. Other vessels running the length of the earthworm send out lateral branches which go to most of the segments.

The crayfish found in lakes and ponds is much bigger and stronger and has many legs, but it cannot leave the water on which it depends for breathing. Unlike the worm and grasshopper, which breathe air through pores on their bodies, the crayfish breathes through *gills*. A gill is a breathing apparatus, like lungs, that takes oxygen out of water instead of from air. The crayfish's gills are in the thorax area. The crayfish also has a new

kind of circulatory system. The simple heart, or throbbing section, has two chambers—one chamber that sucks and a second which pumps. The crayfish's blood system, like that of grasshopper, is an open system.

In the development of circulation, the crayfish was the step before the next major development—the fish.

In fish the heart is a simple one with two chambers that operates in a very large circulatory system.

The fish is a specialized animal, with many organs that need feeding by the blood. It has gills but they are behind its head, inside its body. Its circulation, however, is still in one main direction. The heart receives old blood from the body, pumps it through its two chambers and squirts it out through the second chamber (the ventricle) out through the gills to the body. In the fish's blood, there is also the first mixture of red and white cells.

The frog is the next change in this series. It takes in water through gills during its early life but as an adult breathes air through lungs. Because it needs water to keep its skin

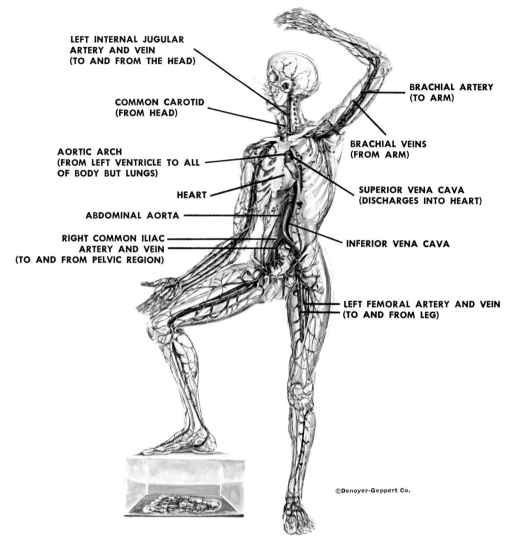

LEFT INTERNAL JUGULAR
ARTERY AND VEIN
(TO AND FROM THE HEAD)

COMMON CAROTID
(FROM HEAD)

AORTIC ARCH
(FROM LEFT VENTRICLE TO ALL
OF BODY BUT LUNGS)

HEART

ABDOMINAL AORTA

RIGHT COMMON ILIAC
ARTERY AND VEIN
(TO AND FROM PELVIC REGION)

BRACHIAL ARTERY
(TO ARM)

BRACHIAL VEINS
(FROM ARM)

SUPERIOR VENA CAVA
(DISCHARGES INTO HEART)

INFERIOR VENA CAVA

LEFT FEMORAL ARTERY AND VEIN
(TO AND FROM LEG)

©Denoyer-Geppert Co.

wet at all times, the frog cannot leave its damp surroundings for very long. Its circulatory system must adjust to these changes.

The frog is quite an improvement on the fish. It has legs and can jump like a grasshopper. And its blood system is a closed circle.

The frog's blood system is really two separate systems that work as one unit. To make this possible, the frog has a three-chambered heart with two auricles (upper chambers) and one ventricle. The three chambers work together to pick up, mix, and circulate two kinds of blood. One kind of blood is called *impure* blood because it contains waste carbon dioxide, CO_2, from the breakdown of digested food, in order to release the energy necessary for cellular activity. This process is called cellular respiration. The other kind of blood is called *pure* blood because waste CO_2 has been removed in the lungs and more oxygen added.

The three-chambered heart, while much more efficient than the one- or two-chambered

heart, does not function as well as the four-chambered heart found in higher animals and humans. The four chambers compose two separate blood systems, making the feeding of body organs more efficient.

The right side of the heart receives impure blood from the veins and pumps it out to be purified in the lungs. The left side of the heart then receives the purified blood and pumps it out through the arteries.

In the mammal circulatory system, the gills have now been replaced by lungs. These organs are protected by a cage (the ribs). A new breathing organ, called the *diaphragm,* has been added. All these work together so that one can jump, fight, hunt—literally do everything the animal ancestors could do and more.

Without the four-chambered heart and the blood circulating system attached to it, man could not live for a second.   L. M.

Circumpolar star see Constellation, Polaris, Star

Cirrhosis (sih-ROE-sis) The liver is an important organ of digestion. Its cells can be injured by infection, by poisonous substances, or by the backflow of bile in the liver following obstruction of the bile ducts. The liver reacts by forming scar tissue. Such a condition is called *cirrhosis.*

There are several types of cirrhosis. The two most common are *portal cirrhosis* and *biliary cirrhosis.* Portal cirrhosis is the most frequent. Scar tissue forms around liver cells injured by poisons. At the same time, clusters of new cells are being formed by the liver. The scar tissue shrinks, forming depressions and valleys around nodules of regenerating cells. In the process, the shrinking liver cuts off its own blood supply and can no longer function. The organ becomes firm and hard. The most common cause is alcohol addiction and neglect of good food and vitamins.

Biliary cirrhosis is usually caused by some obstruction which prevents the flow of bile from the liver to the duodenum. The bile, hampered in its normal course, spills into the blood stream. When such a condition occurs, the body's excrement appears whitish or clay-colored, and the skin appears quite jaundiced, or yellow. B. M. H.

Cirro-cumulus see Clouds

Cirro-stratus see Clouds

Cirrus see Clouds

Citric acid (SIT-rick) Citric acid is found in CITRUS FRUITS, especially lemons. Citric acid gives these fruits their sour taste. It plays an important part in the process which gives humans and animals energy and protection against some diseases.

Today citric acid is made by a process which uses certain types of bacteria and a sugar solution, such as molasses. The citric acid made in this way is used in beverages, candy, medicines, foods, and in many chemical processes.

The chemical formula for citric acid is $C_6H_8O_7 \cdot H_2O$. M. S.
SEE ALSO: ACIDS AND BASES

Citron see Citrus fruits

Citronella Citronella is a large GRASS which supplies a pale yellow oil. This oil is rubbed on the skin to keep insects away.

The crop is cut by hand, and the oil extracted by steam distillation. The flower is small and incomplete, lacking petals and sepals. The dry FRUIT is a caryopsis. Citronella is in the family Gramineae. H. J. C.
SEE ALSO: GRASSES

Citrus fruits Citrus fruits are produced by the most important group of tropical and subtropical fruit trees in the world. They grow on evergreen plants and are acid, pulpy fruits. The best known citrus fruits are the lemon, orange, citron, grapefruit, lime, and kumquat. Some other citrus fruits are the limequat, mandarin orange, pomelo, pummelo, shaddock, tangerine, and tangelo. All citrus fruits are rich in Vitamin C.

Citrus fruits are raised commercially in southern Florida, the Mississippi Delta, the lower Rio Grande Valley, and southern California. This area is sometimes called the *citrus belt.* Frost injures all the citrus trees. The lime is the most tender and the kumquat is the hardiest. Citrus fruits will grow best in well-drained soil. For marketing purposes, many trees are planted together in *groves.*

The semi-tropical *lemon* tree is a small spiny evergreen tree. It grows about 15 feet (4.57 meters) tall. Lemon trees have pale green, shiny, oval leaves and small flowers of a purplish color. The lemon fruit is about 4 inches (10.16 centimeters) long. It is oblong and has a thick yellow skin. The fruit ripens in the winter but is usually stored until the summer season when there is a great demand for lemon juice for cool drinks.

Commercially, the *orange* is the most important of the citrus fruits. It is the fruit of a long-lived evergreen tree. The orange tree is small and has broad, green leaves. The branches are low, and the flowers are white and wax-like. Because of the beauty and fragrance of the orange blossoms, they have long been carried by brides. Oranges are grown in the citrus belt. There are many varieties. The fruit is round, bright orange in color, and contains a pulp which is divided into oblong segments. These are filled with a sugary and refreshing juice, and in most varieties contain several seeds. Seedless oranges, which are the most popular for eating in the United States, are called *navel* oranges.

The *grapefruit* is a large yellow fruit that grows on the tree in bunches or clusters, as grapes do. It derived its name from this similarity. The grapefruit has an acid, juicy pulp that is in segments like those of an orange. Each grapefruit is from 4-7 inches (10.16-17.78 centimeters) in diameter and weighs 1-5 pounds (.45-2.27 kilograms). Grapefruit is a popular breakfast food and is used in salads or for its refreshing juice.

The *lime* tree is a small, tropical, thorny evergreen, grown for its strongly acid fruit. The tree grows about 8 feet (2.44 meters) high. Because of its tenderness to frost it is raised only in the southern tip of Florida and in California. The fruit of the lime resembles the lemon but is green in color.

Kumquats grow on shrubby evergreen trees. They are related to the orange and are grown in the citrus belt of the United States. The kumquat tree grows about 10 feet (3.05 meters) tall and has glossy green leaves and small, white, fragrant flowers. The kumquat is a small aromatic fruit about an inch (2.5 centimeters) in diameter. Whole kumquats are eaten as fresh fruit, or they are made into jelly and jam. Kumquats are the hardiest of all the citrus fruits.

The *citron* is a large, lemon-like citrus fruit whose thick, spongy peel is candied for use in cakes, candies, and other baked foods. The small, spiny, irregular tree or shrub that bears citron is so tender that its cultivation is limited to southern Florida and California.   M.R.L.

SEE ALSO: FRUIT TREES, VITAMINS

Civet Civets, native to Asia and Africa, are related to cats. The animals have weasel-like faces and gray with black fur. A secretion from special glands is used as a perfume base.

SEE: CAT FAMILY

There are many orange groves in Florida, California and Texas

The oranges grow and ripen

The fruit is picked and put into large baskets or boxes

The oranges are sorted according to size

All photos Courtesy Society For Visual Education, Inc.
These oranges are being given a protective coat of wax before shipping

Courtesy Society For Visual Education, Inc.
Horse clam

Clam The clam is a shelled animal *(mollusk)* that lives in sea or fresh water. Its soft body is enclosed in a sac that lines two shells. The shells are hinged by strong muscles that open and close the hard cover.

The clam has a foot-like organ which it uses to burrow in the sand and mud. It has a siphon of two tubes, one to take in water which supplies the animal with oxygen and food, and the other to expel waste. The fleshy part of the clam is edible.

Clams produce eggs in great numbers. The eggs are fertilized in the water by movable sperm. The sexes may be separate or in the same animal (hermaphroditic.)

Clams live along the Atlantic and Pacific coasts, in the Gulf of Mexico, and in the waters around the British Isles.   W. J. K.

Class see Animals, classification of; Plants, classification of

Claw A claw is a sharp NAIL on the finger or toe of an animal. It is made of the same material as the fingernails and toenails of a human. Animals use their claws as weapons to protect themselves and to get food.

All members of the CAT FAMILY, such as lions, tigers and the house cat, use their claws when they attack or are attacked.

PARAKEETS use their claws as hooks when climbing on their cages, but BIRDS OF PREY, such as the eagle, use their claws to kill smaller animals for food.   J. K. K.

Courtesy Society For Visual Education, Inc.

Clay Clay is an earthy material that is composed of tiny particles, most of which are in the crystalline form. Clay results from the chemical breakdown of rocks and minerals. These weathered materials are first transported by running water and then deposited in quiet waters.

Most clays are derived from the mineral *feldspar;* however, other minerals, such as talc, quartz, and mica, may also form clay. Clay, when wet, has an earthy odor and feels quite slippery. Dry clay is soft and has a greasy feel when rubbed. Clay becomes hard when it is fired. It has many uses, such as in making fine china and earthenware, different types of drainage pipes, and as a filter.

One of the more important types of clay is the mineral *kaolinite,* often referred to as KAOLIN. Kaolinite, a china clay, is an *aluminum silicate* which has the chemical formula of $Al_2(Si_2O_5)OH_4$. Its hardness ranges from 2.0 to 2.5, and its specific gravity is about 2.6.

Crystals of kaolinite are very small, almost microscopic. The crystals are six-sided and belong to the *monoclinic system.* This mineral is usually found as a white, earthy substance that is easily crushed. Kaolinite is the result of the weathering of feldspar. When water and carbon dioxide act on common feldspar, chemical and physical changes result. It loses its luster, its cleavage is altered, and it becomes soft and mealy. The kaolinite that is formed may remain where it originally was or it may be transported by running water to the beds of streams, lakes, or oceans, where it is consolidated.   H.S.G.

SEE ALSO: FULLER'S EARTH, KAOLIN, SOIL TYPES

Some uses of clay

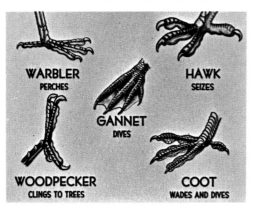

WARBLER
PERCHES

HAWK
SEIZES

GANNET
DIVES

WOODPECKER
CLINGS TO TREES

COOT
WADES AND DIVES

Cleavage

Cleavage (KLEE-vidg) In biology, cleavage is any of the series of divisions by which a fertilized egg develops into a new individual or *embryo.*

The young animal begins life as a fertilized egg. The uniting of the male reproductive cell (sperm) and the female reproductive cell (egg) begins the activity of this new embryo or young animal.

This fertilized egg (ZYGOTE) begins development, but the rate is not the same in all parts. To describe this difference in growth rate, or METABOLISM, certain terms are given for different parts of the egg. The end where concentration of living protoplasm is greatest is called the *animal pole,* while the end where the concentration of food is greatest is called the *vegetal pole.* Natural development is more rapid at the animal pole than at the vegetal pole.

In cleavage the first two divisions, not simultaneously but one following the other, usually cut through the poles of the egg at right angles to each other. The third cleavage cuts the egg between the poles at right angles to the polar axis and a little nearer to the animal pole. All these cleavages result in eight cells, the four at the vegetal end being a little larger than the others.

There are many variations as development continues, but certain general ends are reached even though the manner of attaining them differs in different species of animals. During the latter part of the cleavage period, the cells arrange themselves in the form of a hollow sphere. This is called the *blastula stage.* One side of the blastula moves inward until the walls meet and the embryo is transformed into a double-walled cup or sac called the *gastrula.* The double walls are called germ layers. The outer layer is the *ectoderm;* the inner layer is the *endoderm;* the newly formed cavity is the *primitive gut;* and its opening is the *blastopore.* A middle layer, the *mesoderm,* is eventually formed between the ectoderm and endoderm.

By forming these germ layers, the embryo lays the groundwork for organs. The germ layers continue to develop into various tis-

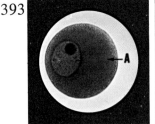

Single-cell stage in a starfish, enlarged 320 times. A is the cytoplasm of the fertilized egg (magnified 320 times)

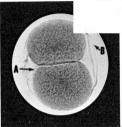

First cleavage of the zygote. A is the divided cell membrane. B, the fertilization membrane, does not divide

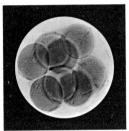

Photo-micrographs by National Teaching Aids, Inc.

Four cells have become eight. The total mass does not change during cleavage

Blastula — the mass has become a hollow ball; differentiation has not started

sues and organs of the body. Each germ layer gives rise to particular organs and tissues.

The ectoderm gives rise to the nervous system, the epidermis, and its derivatives; such as hair, nails, feathers, claws, and hoofs.

The endoderm gives rise to the lining of the digestive and respiratory systems. The glands such as the salivary glands, the liver, and the pancreas are lined with derivatives of the endoderm.

The mesoderm gives rise to the major share of the animal body. Of the mesodermal derivatives, the bones and muscles make up more than half the body weight. The entire circulatory system and lymphatic system (heart, blood, blood vessels, and lymph tubes), the urinary system, the genital organs, the supporting tissues of the digestive and respiratory systems, and the inner layer of the skin are derivatives from the mesoderm.

All embryos are soft delicate structures. They can easily be warped out of shape and deformed if their development is in too rigid an enclosure. They need a soft fluid medium in which to develop. Animals that develop in water have these advantages. In contrast to those that develop in water, embryos that

develop from land-type eggs or within the uteri of mammals, form additional structures known as *extraembryonic membranes.* These membranes lie outside the body of the embryo and function as support and protection. They are used only during the embryonic stage and then discarded. V. V. N.
SEE ALSO: EMBRYOLOGY

Cleft palate Cleft palates result from an incomplete union of the roof of the mouth during its formation before birth.

The roof of the mouth is formed from two sections growing out from both sides. They meet in the center. If union is incomplete, a hole, or cleft, remains in the roof of the mouth. A nasal voice results from air passing through this hole into the *nasal cavity,* which normally would be closed. One quarter of cleft palate cases are combined with a HARELIP. Surgery is corrective. B. M. H.

Helen J. Challand

Clematis

Clematis Clematis is a vine with small white or large purple flowers. Some species are HERBS and do not climb. Flowers may be shaped like stars, vases, or bells depending on the species.

Cliff A cliff is a nearly vertical rock wall, formed when streams, GLACIERS and ocean waves erode away softer rock, leaving harder or more resistant rock standing.

Cliff

Climate Climate is the sum total or average weather of a place on earth. WEATHER is the condition of the atmosphere at a certain time and place. The climate of a region is determined by the records of weather over a long period of time.

Climate is very important as a geographical control. It affects almost all of man's activities. To a large extent, climate is the cause of the natural vegetation and kind of soil a region may have. Because of this, it influences the utilization of the land.

As geographers attempt to classify the climates of earth, they are faced with many different problems. Various proposals have been suggested, but none of them seem to satisfy all of the requirements needed to cover the realm of man's activities. The basic difficulty is that there are hardly any sharp boundaries between climatic zones. Different climatic regions seem to fade gradually into each other. In addition, the atmosphere's general circulation shifts north and south from season to season and from year to year, bringing to different locations on earth first one type of climate and then another. Therefore, a strict classification which separates natural climatic zones is not possible. All dividing lines are, by their very nature, arbitrary. This is even more true when, as in most climatic classifications, the classification is based upon mean values of the climatic elements. Then, too, the choice of combinations of factors used in the classification is often dictated by the specific reason and purposes of the classification rather than by inherent properties of the climate itself.

CONTROLS OF CLIMATE

There are eight important controls of climate to be considered when classifying climates on the basis of temperature and rainfall, which are the main criteria that are used for most systems of climatic classification.

1. *Latitude* (sun)
2. *Land mass* vs. *ocean area*
3. *Seasonal highs and lows*
4. *Winds and air masses*
5. *Cyclonic fronts*
6. *Altitude*
7. *Ocean currents*
8. *Mountain barriers*

Climate largely determines the kind of vegetation to be found in any area. The two maps show how closely the vegetation zones follow climate zones. For example, the eastern section of the United States is humid with regular rainfall, and is warm in summer, cold in winter. This climate favors deciduous trees, which shed their leaves in winter and lie dormant until spring returns. Grasses thrive in almost any climate, but they are especially suited for the subhumid and semidry areas where rainfall is uncertain. Small, fast-growing spiny plants are adapted to growing in dry areas

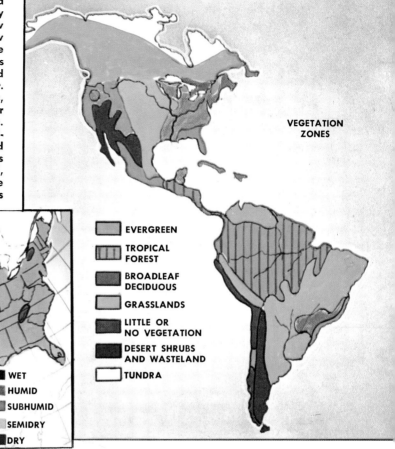

VEGETATION ZONES

EVERGREEN

TROPICAL FOREST

BROADLEAF DECIDUOUS

GRASSLANDS

LITTLE OR NO VEGETATION

DESERT SHRUBS AND WASTELAND

TUNDRA

CLIMATE ZONES

WET

HUMID

SUBHUMID

SEMIDRY

DRY

These controls of climate act on both the elements of temperature and precipitation. Those conditions controlling the temperature characteristics of a region are as follows:

1. The higher the *latitude,* the colder the climate. Increase in latitude also produces small daily temperature ranges with large yearly ranges.

2. The higher the *altitude,* the colder the climate. An increase in altitude causes a decrease in temperature at the average rate of 3.5° F. per 1,000-foot rise (0.6° C. per 100 meters) above sea level. This phenomenon is the *normal adiabatic lapse rate.*

3. *Land masses* and *ocean areas* affect the temperature ranges. Ocean areas have marine climates with small temperature ranges, both daily and yearly. Land areas have continental climates with large ranges. Those land areas at low latitudes will have large daily ranges, while those of high latitudes will have large yearly ranges.

4. Another important factor that affects temperature and temperature ranges is that of *prevailing winds.* The direction from which

they blow and the type of surface over which they have traveled can greatly affect the climate of a region. When winds blow from large bodies of water, temperature ranges are small; when they blow from large land areas, temperature ranges are large.

5. *Mountain barriers* often are the main factor in determining whether winds from distant oceans will modify the climate of a region. As an example, the mountains of the western United States most certainly have a modifying effect on the Great Plains.

6. *Ocean currents* may make the climate of a region warmer or colder than is normal for its latitude. A *warm* ocean current is one that is warmer than the land near which it is passing; a *cold* current is colder than the land it flows past. Ocean currents can also greatly affect the amount of precipitation a region receives annually.

The factors that control the rainfall features of climate may be summarized as follows:

1. The *latitude* of a region may place it in more than one wind or pressure belt during

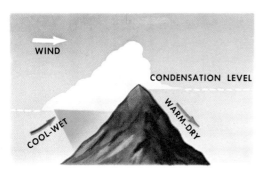

Much of the strength of wind, and most of its moisture, is lost as it passes over a mountain. The side away from wind is warmer and drier

the course of the year. This is especially true of regions that are in the low latitudes of the tropics. As the sun's vertical rays shift north and south in the course of a year, so do most of the wind and pressure belts. This "shift" is often responsible for increasing the *monsoon* effect, which may bring heavy precipitation.

2. Location on the *windward* or *leeward* side of a mountain will mean either more or less rainfall than is normal for the latitude. The windward side of a mountain barrier normally will receive large amounts of precipitation due to *adiabatic* cooling of the air that is

forced to rise over it. Adiabatic cooling results as rising air moves up into regions of lower air pressure, where the air molecules can expand. This results in the condensation of the water vapor, which leads to precipitation. On the leeward side the process is reversed. The descending air moves into areas of higher pressure, which results in warmer air and very little precipitation.

3. Where *prevailing winds* blow from the sea, the areas close to the sea generally receive the most rainfall. Other controls of climate, such as ocean currents, may modify this, however.

4. *Ocean currents* that are much warmer or colder than their adjoining land or water are likely to produce fogs and also have a great influence on the amount of precipitation received. The line where cold and warm water meet is termed a *cold wall*.

SYSTEMS OF CLIMATIC CLASSIFICATION

Most systems of climatic classification are based on two main elements: the average temperature and precipitation of a region. These values take into consideration both average monthly and yearly readings. Some systems use natural vegetation as the basis

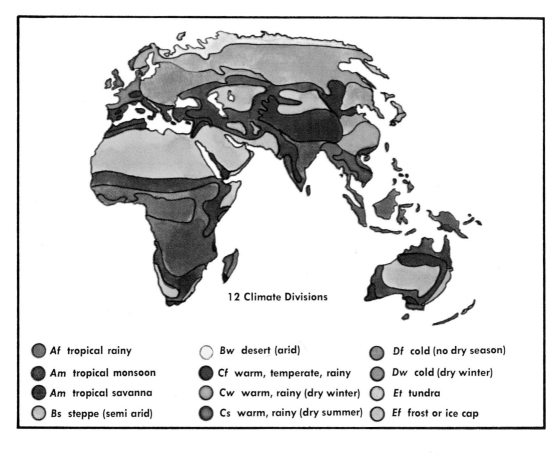

12 Climate Divisions

- **Af** tropical rainy
- **Am** tropical monsoon
- **Am** tropical savanna
- **Bs** steppe (semi arid)
- **Bw** desert (arid)
- **Cf** warm, temperate, rainy
- **Cw** warm, rainy (dry winter)
- **Cs** warm, rainy (dry summer)
- **Df** cold (no dry season)
- **Dw** cold (dry winter)
- **Et** tundra
- **Ef** frost or ice cap

for classification. In 1918, a well-known geographer, Dr. Vladimir Koppen of the University of Austria, proposed a scheme for climatic classification that was based on the elements of temperature, precipitation, and amount of evaporation. Most maps today that show the climates of the earth are based on, or are a modification of, the Koppen system. Koppen used a shorthand description employing the use of capital and lowercase letters. The Koppen system is made up of five major climatic *zones,* which in turn consist of twelve principal climatic *types.* The five major zones are as follows:

A. *Tropical rainy climates:* These are also referred to as tropical forest climates where the coldest month is over 64.4° F. (18° C.). The temperature line was chosen because, when cool-season temperatures are below 64.4° F. (18° C.) some tropical plants do not thrive.
B. *Dry climates:* This is the zone of the warm and cold deserts and the steppes of the world. The degree of potential evaporation that may exceed the annual rainfall is the limiting criterion. Since there is not a water surplus, headwaters of streams are not found in these areas.
C. *Warm temperate climates:* These are humid climates with mild winters. The warmest months are over 64.4 F. (18° C.), but the coldest months are always below 50° (10° C.) and may range below freezing.
D. *Snow climates:* These are humid climates with cold winters. Like warm temperature climates, summers range over 64.4° F. (18° C.). However, they are shorter and cooler than warm temperate climates.
E. *Polar climates:* Cold climates, with the average temperature of the warmest month being below 50° F. (10° C.). These climates have no true summer.

Each of these major zones are subdivided on the basis of the amount and distribution of rainfall. Dry, warm, and snow climates are further subdivided to provide a more exact description.

The twelve principal climatic types, with their subdivisions and additional notations, are as follows:

1. *Af* tropical rainy climate
2. *Am* tropical savanna climate
3. *Am* tropical monsoon climate
4. *BS* steppe (semiarid) climate
5. *BW* desert (arid) climate
6. *Cf* warm, temperate, rainy climate without dry season
7. *Cw* warm, temperate, rainy climate with dry winter
8. *Cs* warm, temperate, rainy climate with dry summer
9. *Df* cold, snow-forest climate without dry season
10. *Dw* cold, snow-forest climate with dry winter
11. *ET* tundra climate
12. *EF* frost or icecap climate

In the Koppen system, additional shorthand letter notations are used to provide a more complete description of some of the climatic types. These include notations that indicate climates are due to altitude, cold or hot deserts and steppes, areas of frequent fog, and many other items. The system does not, however, take into consideration such conditions as lake breezes and other local weather phenomena. H. S. G.

SEE ALSO: AFRICA, ASIA, AUSTRALIA, EUROPE, NORTH AMERICA, SOUTH AMERICA

Climax community

A climax community is reached when a group of living organisms in a particular environment have become stable. A balanced aquarium or terrarium are climax communities.

There is constant *succession* until certain plants become dominant. The community maintains equilibrium. It stays this way unless upset by fire, man, or disease. In some areas the oak-hickory community is a climax while in others it is the beech-maple. Grass is the climax vegetation in the prairies of central North America. H.J.C.

Cloaca

(klo-ACHE-uh) The cloaca is a chamber, opening to the outside, into which the rectum, excretory, and reproductive ducts open.

In all mammals except the small egg-laying group (*monotremes*), the cloaca forms only in the embryo. By the time of birth, three separate openings have formed. J. C. K.

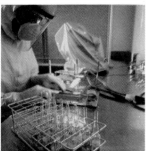

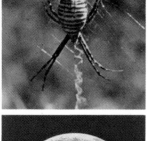

Conversion Factors
to Metric Measurement

Length

1 inch = 25.4 millimeters (mm) exactly
1 inch = 2.54 centimeters (cm) exactly
1 foot = 0.3048 meters (m) exactly
1 yard = 0.9144 meters (m) exactly
1 mile = 1.609344 kilometers (km) exactly

Area

1 square inch = 6.4516 square centimeters (cm^2) exactly
1 square foot = 0.092903 square meters (m^2)
1 square yard = 0.836127 square meters (m^2)
1 square acre = 0.404686 hectares (ha)
1 square mile = 2.58999 square kilometers (km^2)

Cubic Measure

1 cubic inch = 16.387064 cubic centimeters (cm^3) exactly
1 cubic foot = 0.0283168 cubic meters (m^3)
1 cubic yard = 0.764555 cubic meters (m^3)

US Liquid Measure

1 fluid ounce = 29.5735 milliliters (ml)
1 fluid ounce = 0.2957 deciliters (dl)
1 pint = 0.473176 liters (l)
1 gallon = 3.78541 liters (l)

US Dry Measure

1 pint = 0.550610 liters (l)
1 bushel = 35.2391 liters (l)

Weight

1 grain = 0.0647989 grams (g)
1 ounce = 28.3495 grams (g)
1 pound = 0.453592 kilograms (kg)
1 short ton = 0.907185 metric tons (t)
1 UK ton = 1.01605 metric tons (t)

Temperature

To convert Fahrenheit to Centigrade (Celsius) complete the following
equation. $(F° - 32) \times 5 \div 9 = C°$